I lick my
cheese

I lick my cheese

AND OTHER NOTES FROM THE FRONTLINE OF
FLAT-SHARING

Oonagh O'Hagan

sphere

www.flatmatesanonymous.com

sphere

First published in Great Britain in 2007 by Sphere

A CIP catalogue record for this book is available from the British Library.

ISBN 978-1-84744-128-7

Printed and bound in Italy

Sphere
An imprint of
Little, Brown Book Group
Brettenham House
Lancaster Place
London WC2E 7EN

A Member of the Hachette Livre Group of Companies

www.littlebrown.co.uk

Contents

Foreword

Most of us at some time in our life will share a flat with somebody we don't know as well as we think – perhaps as a student, leaving home for the first time, or maybe after coming out of a long relationship. It's a fact of modern life – a rite of passage even. If you have shared a flat with strangers or, more usually, friends, you will recognise the pattern: people who you think are perfectly normal can quickly turn out to be completely insane. Weird habits, idiosyncrasies and obsessions begin to emerge, such as a preoccupation with food labelling or an overzealous use of bleach. And then the notes start to appear.

These little notes range from the tedious to the ridiculous, the amusing to the downright disturbing. Each day can reveal a new issue or problem – and a new note.

As a designer, I'm fascinated by people's behaviour, particularly the way they express feelings and beliefs. A note can tell you so much about a person – from the choice of paper (the back of a fag packet or a pristine new sheet of A4), to the words underlined or put in capitals, to the drawings and doodles that illustrate their requests, demands and complaints. The notes capture everything from lunacy to genius.

Over the years a number of my own flatmates have resorted without embarrassment to the written word. One in particular seemed to communicate solely via notes. These notes became increasingly frequent and terrifying, soon escalating into a full-blown catfight – but one that was never openly discussed or even acknowledged. Small talk and general niceties were still exchanged in an apparently natural manner as we passed each other in the hall, but this was the same woman who frantically wrote on the back of a microwave-meal packet:

Please don't soak my stuff that's made out of wood – it bends and cracks them when the fibres get full of water. Cheers!

How to react to this? How to feel anything other than utterly baffled, if not unsettled?

As these silent brawls continued between us, ranging from the amount of space my food took up in the fridge to a mythological vendetta against a boyfriend of hers I had never met, I realised we were not alone in this note writing. Soon friends and acquaintances were telling me about ongoing fights involving messages such as:

Someone has eaten my pasta, I'm hungry.

and,

Out of my thirty multi-vitamins and iron tablets I have only had approximately fifteen. Unless you want to be blamed for me becoming anaemic I suggest that whoever has been taking them replace them.

Everyone seemed to be in the midst of either being accused or accusing others of thieving shampoo, squatting in cupboard space, *deliberately* clogging up toilets and other such weirdness.

As I researched further, I realised the most alarming and irritating were not the aggressive, accusing notes, but the instructive, even enthusiastic ones. I include within this category the flatmate who always left out cake and asked for comments on how to make it 'even more yummy'. If that wasn't nauseating enough, there was the friend's flatmate who instead of writing notes just left photocopied extracts from the Bible around the house. And as for the shocking number of people who resort to *typing* their words of wisdom ...

What does this all mean?

When you start to look into it, *everything* gets discussed through these notes. Love, anger, jealousy, food, hatred – they all feature. And not only is the subject matter random and strange, but so are the items that are written on: the back of a bill, in the margarine and, worst of all, on the walls in snot. But the one thing that links all the writers is the need to be heard without confrontation.

I started to collect these notes. As I did so, I realised that not only was this a way to get inside and snoop around people's flats, but it was a fascinating and intriguing way of getting inside their minds. Suddenly a book was emerging – one with secrets, fights and scandals, but all based on actual people and events. In some instances, this book champions those who just want the decent thing done, but I cannot deny that at times it is also a work of revenge. After all those years of torment and torture inflicted by the range of freaks, frumps and sometimes friends we've had to share our personal space with, here was a chance to fight back. But the note writers should not be too upset; after all, it is also a celebration of their work.

From the mundane to the ridiculous, these messages probably say more about the way we share our lives and relate to other people than a whole library of psychology studies. Behind those few words, scribbled in frustration, rage, desperation and occasionally goodwill, lies a whole story. You could be pretentious and claim they're almost like poetry, or you could just say they're very, very funny and a little bit disturbing. Either way, I hope you enjoy reading them as much as I enjoyed collecting them. I should point out that not only did I receive the actual notes but often some (dodgy quality) photos of them in situ, so this is to forewarn you about some of the amateur photography in the book! If you feel that you have a note that is worthy of scrutiny, you can submit it to, and keep up to date with all new notes on: www.flatmatesanonymous.com

Go there and join the virtual flat.

I pay the rent.
What do you do?

PARTIES, LIVING TOGETHER AND
OTHER NOTES FROM THE LIVING ROOM

The living room is a common room: a communal space full of people with nothing in common. Different creeds and cultures reluctantly come together over a soap or a TV dinner. TV is often the main hub of a living room but, unlike the edited 'reality' on TV, here all the fights are real and there is no off switch when you get sick of the puerile arguments.

My favourite notes come from situations where the living room has slowly morphed into another room – usually a bedroom – the scene of embarrassing clinches, boyfriends slowly becoming permanent fixtures on couches and other behaviour that should be reserved for rooms with locks. Talking of locks, when a living room starts being the popular venue for any type of personal grooming (see note on toenail clippings) you know that you have the potential catalyst for a flat meeting. Sadly, it is difficult to take a flat meeting at all seriously. Very rarely have I heard of this kind of organised discussion working well. In fact, the only time it seems to work is when interrogating, sorry, *interviewing* potential new flatmates; fresh meat to dissect and prod, this appears to be the one thing that can bring an otherwise fraught and disjointed flat household together.

I hang my head in shame even thinking about flatmate interviewing as I have found myself part of these character assassinations. The film *Shallow Grave* portrayed this scenario very well. It is horribly entertaining to watch your victim squirm as they attempt to sell themselves to you. There are some people you know you are not going to get on with almost immediately. It can be their smile, handshake or cheeky wink, but more often it is their hobbies that are the clinchers for straight rejection. I have personally rejected a perfectly nice young gentleman from New Zealand. I wasn't totally impressed with his answers or aesthetics (shallow but true – if you are going to see them every day it is an added bonus if they are easy on the eye) but everything seemed to be going decently until he said that what he had really been looking for was somewhere with a huge dick. He continued through the noise of our all female household's jaws hitting the floor, telling us that there was nothing like a big dick and sunshine to make sure you slept well. It was only when he said that he could see why there weren't many big dicks in London to *lie on* that the penny dropped. Lie on? Where were these amazing creatures that you could lie on? Oh God, he means *deck*, a deck, oh, thank God, a deck, a sundeck. Our Kiwi gentleman looked baffled about why two potential flatmates had hurried out of the living room with wry smiles followed by muffled laughter. I was left to show our deck lover the door, explaining to him we would have a think and let him know once we had interviewed everyone who was interested in the room. I also pointed out that I too was disappointed that we didn't have a big dick in the flat.

Curiously, it is when the interrogators shift to being the inter-rogated that another flatmate-bonding moment occurs. As potential new recruits ask how much the bills are or comment that the facilities aren't very good, it is difficult not to become defensive of your humble communal areas. How dare a complete stranger turn her snooty nose up at your living space. The area you have despised and the people you have bitched about suddenly become your domain and your comrades. What is this viewer's problem with the living room? Don't they like the squatter on the couch or the toenail clippings? Don't they want to join our commune? Big decks to them.

You have written me a cheque for the water bill for £42.13, but it's actually £41.13. Would you like me to give you the £1.00 back, or would you prefer I ripped up the cheque and you can write another cheque for the right amount?

This was given to me by a friend who said that they told this flatmate, who was a prolific note writer, to go treat themselves with the extra pound.

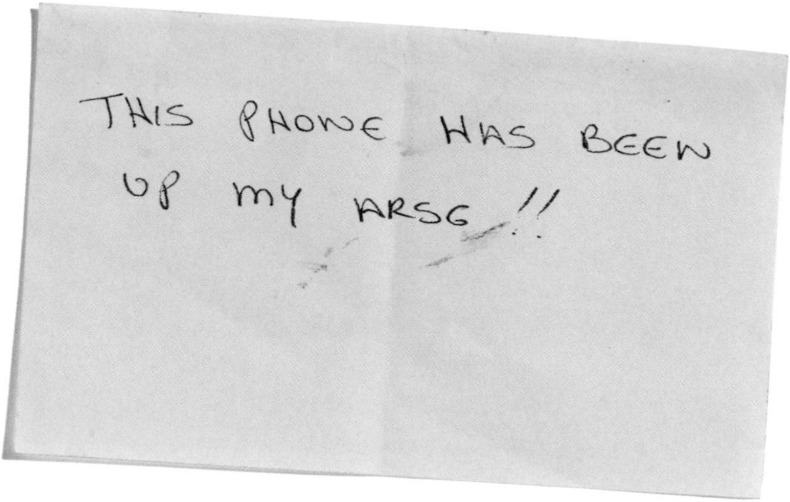
THIS PHONE HAS BEEN
UP MY ARSE !!

This came from a woman who had been away from her flat and who had allocated the morning after her return to tidying up before her parents visited that afternoon. As she entered the flat, she walked in to find, judging from the general disarray, that a very successful party had recently ended. With a distinct sense of panic setting in, and realising that the tidying-up operation in advance of the parental visit was going to be a bit more intense than she had envisaged, she entered the kitchen with some trepidation. She was not wrong to be wary; on the kitchen floor, lying face down in a suit, was a gentleman she had never seen before. That was not the most disturbing part of it, however. The phone lying next to him had a Post-it® note attached to it that read: *This phone has been up my arse.* When she gave me the note, she explained that the nameless man and the flatmates who were the culprits for the party managed to clean the whole flat and the visiting parents were none the wiser. The only evidence that anything ever happened that night is the note.

Dear Binky

You will be glad to know that my grandfather's visit to Edinburgh was a success. Not only did he manage to get to the top of our stairs alive, but when he did so + settled into our sofa with a cup of tea, he was enlivened by the sight of your 2 foot long bong which you had thoughtfully left on display on the coffee table.

I shall remember to be as equally as thoughtful upon your next grand-parental visit.

Mark

'X' sounds like he could possibly maybe perhaps be a smoker of marijuana. Of course, I might be totally wrong, and I am by no means saying someone like X would ever have inhaled. I do in fact understand that he had actually cleaned up the flat (even leaving out some fancy tea), but somehow had managed not to notice his favourite memento from Morocco ...

Dear ████████

Hope you dont mind me clearing your damp wank rag off the table. Its just that i was expecting friends round for dinner and they probably think that its a fucking disgrace that someone would have the audacity to wank in my living room than wander off like they'd just finished work for the evening. This note serves to close your grubby little episode. Its also your notice to leave the house. In the meantime, put one foot wrong and I'll set fire to your stuff, not even kidding.

████████

Sometimes the horror of a face-to-face confrontation is totally understandable – and this is one of them. This note appears to want to shame this person even further, he possibly not having been shamed enough following the discovery that he'd turned an idle moment into an opportunity to explore sexual pleasure ... in the living room. Pleasuring oneself in the communal area might be OK if people would at least be courteous enough to dispose of the evidence. Worryingly, this seems, pardon the awful pun, to come up quite often.

Subtle yet effective.

WHATEVER YOU DO.
NEVER LET THE
———
BAILIFFS IN !

Ah, now this sounds familiar. I had a 'bailiff incident' once. I had
been writing cheques for the bills to another flatmate. Little did
I know the flatmate was cashing them but rather than paying
the bills was spending the money on a mixture of vices. The first
I knew of this was when the doorbell rang and the bailiffs were at
the door. Knowing how these things work, I realised that if I let
them in they would take anything that wasn't bolted down. The
flatmate who had taken the money instead of paying the bills
wasn't the brightest spark, seeing as he thought I wouldn't find
out. (Later on, I found lots of red reminder letters hidden in his
room – very mature.)

Need it to go, Home And
Do some work.

(I Do apologize if,
Wrote your name
wrong).

"I Have a tiny dixlexia."

~~Vincent Jacques~~

X:

Living with someone whose first language is not yours can be a challenge. Living with someone whose first language is not yours and has dyslexia can be a bit of a mission. It is difficult enough to decide whether you should point out grammatical errors, without the added element of them being foreign and their sole reason for living in the country being to learn the language, but you can get into an emotional minefield if you start thinking they have difficulties in their own language as well as their second. I can only guess that being dyslexic is international, but does that mean you are dyslexic in every language you learn? Just as I find speaking German easier than speaking French, is it possible our mother tongue might not be the one that is best suited for us? Whatever the answer, this person has recognised they need to go home and do some work. Personally, I am impressed if anyone can speak any language well, including their own.

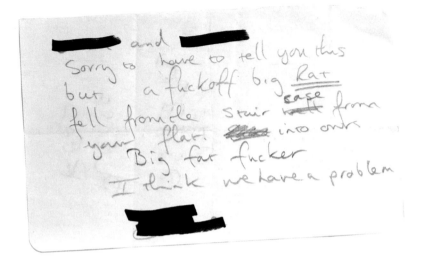

Sorry to have to tell you this
but a fuckoff big Rat
fell from the stair case from
your flat into ours
Big fat fucker
I think we have a problem

They're watching you, they're round every corner. Yes, rodents and other pests. According to that centre of all useless and dubious statistics (the Internet) there are three rats to every one person in London. You thought you only had two flatmates … maybe you have a few more who are even less sociable.

You are a lying sack of shit. A
38 year old man who can't pay his
rent on time ... fucking pathetic. And
a liar. Don't think you can treat me
like the shit you treat the flaky bitches
hanging around the house. Start paying your
rent on time or get the fuck out.

I'm sensing anger ...

YOU KNOW, THAT I KNOW THAT YOU KNOW THAT I KNOW THAT YOU TOOK IT... SO GIVE IT BACK

The fact that the 'it' goes undefined makes this note terrifying. It's all smoke and mirrors, winks and nods. This is the kind of message that the mafia would leave for a victim as the first chance to pay up before getting to wear the not-so-fashionable concrete shoes.

Bob

Its not that
i've forgotten your
birthday — I was
out celebrating
it66 xxx.

You can't help liking this character, a bit of a lovable rogue.
Apologising, but having far too good a time to ever really be
sorry. Bless.

... when you need her? Is this a last-gasp attempt to find yourself somewhere else to stay? Has Kirsty become the patron saint of flatmates? Where are you, blessed Kirsty?

Here's a stamp. Write to your mum. She keeps calling.

Mums everywhere, we feel your pain. The world is divided into those who phone their mums and those who don't. I know a guy who used to phone his mum once, sometimes twice a day, ending with 'I love you so much'. Jesus. While some people have an Oedipus complex, others have such little contact that when their mums do see them, they refer to it as 'sightings'.

When flat-sharing works out it can be great as you have an extended social circle, even an extended family. How nice to have everyone rooting for you.

hey am a bit depressed all mall.
blah blah same old. Plus have shit
loads to do. BK are by the tv.
Do you wanna go halves? Nice
pasta. Feanyl may not be able
to hang out with you. Hun.
Will work my bs off tnr. May
not be ~~able~~ back
back at night
time .....
Have a good
run!

XX

plus I wore
the vodka
skirt out !!!!

Moving?

Wrongly addressed?

TWUL 902(07/05)

This note initially could be overlooked, as it is the PS that is the main point. The vodka skirt? I did some research into the writer of this note. Apparently the 'vodka skirt' was bought under the influence. In the cold light of day it was a rather garish garment, so wearing the vodka skirt was seen as the start of a seriously kamikaze night out.

Sharing your space can be a real skill but sharing amenities can just be frustrating. We are essentially selfish creatures and, let's face it, most of us think what we say is much more important than what anyone else says. It is always other people that talk 'pap' on the phone. So yeah, get the hell off the phone! Though who says pap? Maybe this lot should be disconnected.

Rent. Often the root of all evil in a flat-share. All is well until money gets involved. The strange thing is, there is always one person in the flat who understands that paying the rent is a condition of living there and others for whom the connection is not so clear. The result is that the former organises everything for the latter, which similarly to the cleaning-obsessive scenario (see bathroom section), suits the lazy rent-dodging bastard of a flatmate just fine.

Well I spoke to none other
than Ringo Starr (!) - He very
comfortingly ran me through
various procedures & eventually
I was connected! (via the yellow cable)
    It was rather overwhelming
that he calmly knew so much!
    I was too grateful to bother
him about anything else.
    I have tomor afternoon off so
will do some rooter research!

        β.

I love this note because, once you understand the background to it, it actually makes sense, but until then it sounds totally ham bonkers. The call was to an Internet helpline, the assistant for which was a Mr Starr whose nickname had obviously become Ringo – thus the comments about him knowing his stuff and yellow cable. It is not a euphemism for anything else.

You have washed, you have vacuumed and you have tidied. You have piled up 'stuff' to be returned to rightful owners and rightful rooms. It is the only thing you ask after slaving away removing mould from bathrooms and descaling kettles. Some days pass and still the piles of unclaimed articles sit at the bottom of the stairs gathering dust. You eventually have to write a note to explain what to do with the items. This is when you should really leave a note explaining where the door is and how to leave, unless you want to remain a doormat.

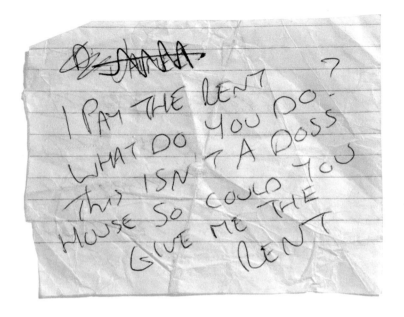

Existing can be pretty difficull in these cut-throat times but even more so when you seem to be a host lo a parasite. This is one of those moments when if you were requested to fill in a form asking you if you had any dependants you would be inclined to say, yes, all my flatmates.

Go to yoga together
you might like it,
I know you have been
feeling a bit insecure
and down lately —
this might chirrup you,
it will be FUN

Well-meaning, but I can't help wondering whether the person who received this note really wanted to be reminded, as they walked into their flat after a hard day, that everybody knew they'd been 'feeling a bit insecure and down lately'.

Hey Ann, I have my suspicions that the landlady is letting herself in when we are out. Some magazines have been moved + I'm sure some of my hobnobs gone!! Is that not against the law?!? (letting yourself in, not eating hobnobs!) do you think you could ask your dad what he thinks. I might get a lock for my door. Will talk to you proper about it this eve.

I suppose it must be very difficult not to have a look if you have the ability – in the same way if someone leaves a diary out it is very difficult not to have a peek. Once a landlord starts this kind of behaviour they can become nonchalant. You start by letting yourself into the flat. No one notices, so you move on to letting yourself in and having a quick read of the magazines. Again, nobody notices. Before you know it you're having baths and eating HobNobs wearing their pants. I don't know the conclusion to this note. I don't know if the landlady really was letting herself in. There are lots of urban myths about tenants finding spy cameras behind mirrors but I have never heard any about HobNob thieves. It should definitely be illegal, though – HobNobs are great.

Dear C, mrs L came in today and I think she has realised that we have built a wall to divide the living room. As we thought, the story about it being a canvas for your art didn't convince her and she is really pissed off. Tried to tell her it was temporary but she could see it was bolted to the floor. Is it too late to tell your friend they might not be able to move in? O

If I had only seen the note I would not have believed this but I had the privilege of seeing this wall-building with my own eyes. With rents being so high, the more people you can fit into a property the better. Adding one more room can make a huge difference to bills, council tax and rent. It is not uncommon to change a living room into a bedroom, but it is quite uncommon to build a wall down the centre of the living room. It is also utterly illegal and dangerous, not to mention smelly, as suddenly you have no way of letting air circulate around a room. The urgency for this room was explained to me. A flatmate's fiancé was coming to stay from abroad so, suddenly, having a big communal sleeping space for two girls was not going to be quite as practical with a male in the mix. Unless they wanted to get into some seriously sordid voyeurism, a partition seemed to be the only answer to these eager and industrious flatmates. Getting plasterboard etc into the flat without raising suspicion was going to be difficult and that is where the canvas-for-art excuse came from. It apparently worked for a while, but eventually, as the 'art' didn't seem to change or move, the wall was discovered for what it was and pulled down. The funniest part of the story is that they were all architects.

Though I am grateful for moving my stuff — there is a LOT missing. 2 jackets (the leather one you liked), CDs AND a teapot. I don't suppose you know where they would have 'gone' ??

Being admired and having your taste in music appreciated is very flattering. Not so great is your clothes and music being liked so much that they get stolen. Things going missing and walking out the door of flat-shares is a horrible and common problem. It's particularly difficult to prove but even more difficult to believe that someone is lying straight to your face. A similar anecdote was told to me by a flatmate who realised money was going missing from his room. When he came home early one day, he walked into his room to find another flatmate helping himself to money from his money tin. At being caught red-handed, the thief said, 'I needed it, and you had it.' If you are bold enough to go into a room and steal, you are going to have no problems lying about it. It is when they wear the clothes in front of you that it gets a bit galling.

I called Ben to see
if he was going
to collect the rest
of his stuff
including 3 suits
and he said
no just leave
them!! Don't you

think that is
totally weird?
I will take them
to Oxfam
tomorrow.

Some people are heathen slobs. When this attribute is combined with rich parents and/or lots of available cash, it can lead to the phenomenon of 'too posh to wash'. In this instance, it was too posh, lazy and drunk to go and collect a whole wardrobe full of clothes. I guess starting afresh may be cheaper than moving everything to your new abode.

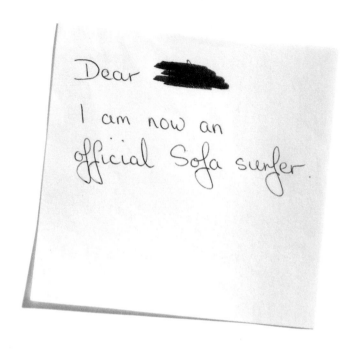

Dear ▓▓▓

I am now an official Sofa surfer.

We have all been here. Something goes wrong, the flat falls through and you don't find anywhere quickly enough. There are endless possibilities why one becomes a citizen of the front room of a good mate. Waking up surrounded by people watching the telly and living out of a bag is a horrible transient phase. This phase exists to make you appreciate your room when you get it, no matter how much of a shoebox it is. It is always better than being a sofa surfer.

There's a coffee cup ring on my Screamadelica CD. I definitely wouldn't do it. Explain.

This is the fate I think all CDs eventually face. With the introduction of MP3-players the life-span of CDs looks like it's going to get increasingly short. Fact is, they were always short anyway. Granted, putting hot drinks on them is no way to treat them but mysterious scratches and jumps evolve from just looking at them. Anyway, have you ever tried to go for a jog with a portable CD-player? It's like having someone with a bad stammer shouting at you the whole way. I say hurrah for the death of the CD – it was crap all along, even when we saw it on *Tomorrow's World*.

MK14 6DY.

Ask before you borrow my
stuff!! — my skirt is totally
stretched after you have shoved
it over your fat arse. You are
one of the most SELFISH people I
have ever met

This note never ceases to make me laugh. I think it is the image of finding something on the floor of your room that looks more reminiscent of a long elastic band than a skirt that makes it so funny; the original pattern completely strained, the garment now resembling Munch's *The Scream*, all stretched and distorted. The owner doubtless put on the offending garment only for it to immediately sag and fall to her knees like a pair of knickers whose elastic had gone. It is also funny that there must have been some denial about body shape. The 'stretcher' probably says she is a size 10 when she is closer to a size 20. She once got a single boob into a size-10 boob tube, thus she now claims to be a size 10. I confess to doing this myself (making the claim, not the boob squeeze). I have walked out of a changing room looking like a sausage because I desperately wanted to get into a smaller-sized dress, breathing shallowly as all effort is put into sucking in the stomach, clenching buttocks and using as little space in my lungs as possible. Men do it too, belting trousers under their belly rather than round it. I can't help thinking well of the 'stretcher'. She didn't care – she just wanted to wear something nice for a night out even if it meant it would be like a long piece of filo pastry by the time she had finished with it.

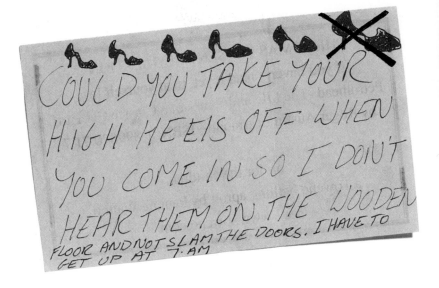

COULD YOU TAKE YOUR HIGH HEELS OFF WHEN YOU COME IN SO I DON'T HEAR THEM ON THE WOODEN FLOOR AND NOT SLAM THE DOORS. I HAVE TO GET UP AT 7 AM

The trend for laminated and wooden floors must have led to an increase in the sales of slippers. One of my friends never recovered from watching a work colleague come to her flat and walk all over her wooden floor in her high heels. One of the tips of the heels had come off leaving what looked like bullet holes all over the beautifully polished and newly laid floor. (The situation got even worse when she pushed back the sofa to get a better view of the TV and left a deep scar in the wood.) It is a no-win situation though: heels equal noise and being accused of doing *Riverdance* above your neighbours' heads. The alternative of wearing slippers is not very attractive and an accident waiting to happen. One quick move on your precious wooden floor and you suddenly find yourself lying concussed and prostrate on your tongue and groove.

This is a lovely idea that never ever works. 'We will all put money in the pot for things like cleaning products and bin bags.' Hmm, when it comes to emptying the pot and counting the money, it is generally thirteen pence and an old button. Even worse is when you have been enthusiastically contributing and when you empty it there is definitely less money than you put in, never mind the amount there should be. There is always someone who decides that 'essential household products' includes several Bacardi and Cokes!

I Don't know why when you are in
the flat all day you have to practise your
guitar at night if I hear the theme from
hill street blues one more time while I am
trying to get to sleep I will mash up your
bloody guitar at night. blues theme alright?
Paul

Noise pollution is a growing nuisance and one that is actually
quite difficult to prove. It is not just confined to living spaces;
suddenly 'muzak' is everywhere. When you are put on hold, as
you enter a lift or as you do your shopping, you find yourself
having no choice but to listen to appalling music. I feel sorry for
the shop assistants who are subjected to CDs on loop – Christmas
must be hellish. Listening to others practising music is even
more painful. Unaccomplished and repetitive, it jars and stops.
You hear the muffled noises of a good song being murdered.
You will the player to get past that one troublesome chord as
listening to it one more time might make you go through there
and turn their guitar into kindling. Poor Paul.

Could you stop writing your very hostile "mine" and "fuck off" labels on everything. Don't know if you have some insecurity problems, but I can assure you I don't want anything of yours.

— —

Living in several different flat-shares can leave you emotionally scarred and paranoid. In trying to nip any future problems in the bud this flatmate has been somewhat over-zealous and abusive with labelling their items. Some grocery abuse had obviously taken place previously: garlic assaulted, cereal kidnapped. They are just looking after their property. I am just glad guns are still illegal here.

These little yellow chicken things are slightly creepy and this one looks as though it has been hanged from the door. Not so much a celebration of new life as a satanic chicken sacrifice. A nice play on words though.

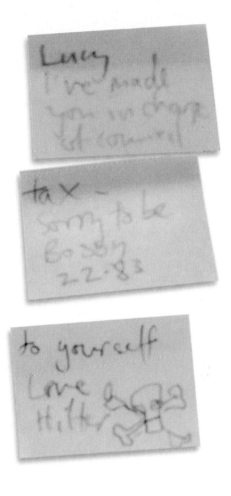

I suppose you could argue that Hitler was very organised and good at giving orders. I just wouldn't necessarily want him as a flatmate. That goes for most fascist leaders.

mosquito

Essentially this is not a note, but I wanted to include it as it speaks volumes. Waking up to find that your body has been treated like a canteen by hungry mosquitoes can be very alarming. Your skin is like the surface of the moon with different areas targeted for blood siphoning. Mosquitoes wouldn't have been the first pest to spring to my mind as being a bane to residents of the UK – I would have thought mice are public enemy numero uno. Such clever rodents: when you do actually catch them, you realise how small, harmless and cute they are. You forget how many of their droppings you have probably eaten in your 'fruit and flakes' cereal. Did you really think the cereal companies had just felt a bit more generous and put more raisins in your muesli? Hell no, look at the tiny gnaw marks on your packet and you will realise you have been wading your way through oats and mouse poo. Ah well, it's all fibre. But back to the tiny insect bloodsuckers – when they get in at night you can understand someone's glee at killing them. It's not quite a stag's head on a wall but a mosquito on a piece of card is still a very satisfactory kill and is the one example of hunting I can sympathise with.

I know this might seem petty, but your domination on what we watch on TV is really depressing me. Watching reruns of the OC which is just an excuse for you to look at nubile young (too young!) girls is not how I want to spend my Saturday mornings. I can take a joke, but hiding the remote controls was really immature!

Immature but probably very funny. As a female, I find many programmes on TV pretty depressing but at least they make some vague attempt at having a storyline. Some other countries seem to have nothing but beauty contests (interestingly only the bikini round) on every channel all the time. OK, so the last thing you want to see in the morning is someone half your age with skin so taut you could bounce fifty-pence pieces off her belly, but the key to living together is compromise. If you can't compromise, get rid of the cable channels and take the batteries out of the remote.

Oh dear! I passed but Apparently my essay 'lacked pace', so did I once I finished. Thank you for the notes and moral support on my all nighter.

Many of the notes I receive are from students and, as I occasionally teach, I often get the note and the background story with it. This is a typical student scenario and one I cannot condemn as I remember doing several 'all nighters'. No matter how many times you plan and make work schedules you find yourself frantically typing away at 3am. I now know this is the way I work and, instead of lying to myself that I will do an hour a night, I build the all nighter into my week. I know I will be tired, grumpy and stressed, but then there is the adrenalin rush and the 'thrill' of the pressure – it took me a while to realise it was for these very reasons I did end up doing my work at the last minute. What we can see from this note is that many others are most productive when in full panic mode. People show amazing feats of strength and courage under adverse conditions, and this is my theory for the all nighter. Twenty-four-hour garages across the country must make a killing around revision time.

Not sure what I think about your interview technique, your point about being "more relaxed" might work for you but I cant help thinking my interview would have gone better without the green.

Dos and don'ts in interviews can be very misleading. For instance, I was once told that if they offer you a drink *do not* take it, as if you are nervous your interviewer will hear a cup rattle or see your hand shaking. I was then told *do* take a drink, as it will give you something to do with your hands. Handshakes should be firm, but what about placing your other hand on top, giving up for a high five or punching the air? And that's even before you move on to the difficult subjects. Salaries, for example – aim high or be realistic? Before you even go in the door you've got sweat clinging to your shirt and have developed a speech impediment. This note shows the lengths some individuals will go to calm their nerves and contains the clear lesson never to listen to anyone else's advice. Going to an interview drunk or, as with this character, drugged ('green' being marijuana for those pretending not to know), I wouldn't have thought is the best start. The fact the interviewee listened to this clown and actually 'smoked the green' does not mark him out as the most employable character. His judgement seems somewhat blurred and getting blurrier.

TO ALL YOU GOOD MEN,
I DO NOT RECOMMEND DOING CHASERS AFTER WORK
TIL 2AM IN A LOCK IN WITH THE LOCALS AT
THE 'TAVERN'. UNLESS YOU WANT TO WAKE UP,
FULLY DRESSED IN YOUR SUIT (AND BROGUES)
WITH NO IDEA WHERE YOUR BRIEFCASE IS.
I'M OFF TO SPEND THE DAY TRYING TO WORK
OUT HOW I GOT HOME AND WHERE MY BAG IS.
THANKFULLY NO CALLING CABS FOR BARMAIDS
THIS MORNING!   LUKE.

Another note full of regret, lamenting the side effects of common vices. This behaviour is bad enough when you live on your own – the dark depression of waking up with no idea what you did the night before, but aware that the result feels like a brace squeezing your head. For this individual it is made a thousand times worse by the fact he has an audience. An audience that, judging by this note, is happy to remind him of the different waifs and strays he has not only socialised with but lured back to his stale room. Luke doesn't get much sympathy seeing as the female is known only as 'barmaid' – perhaps she had a lucky escape. And perhaps he should stick to the soft drinks next time.

I have decided to move in with my freind Caroline. I would move straight away but I think it is only right to give you time to find someone else — though you have never ever considered me. I expect to get my whole deposit back (£360) — if not more! I should have been paid to live here!!.

Theresa.

Washed-out, worn-out, abused, tired, poor girl. And the irony of her name – is this Mother Theresa? I wonder, did Mother Theresa flat-share before going out to Calcutta? This girl sounds as though she had a pretty miserable time. I also get the impression she never saw her deposit and the other flatmates only noticed she had gone when they realised the washing up hadn't been done for several months. This girl needs to go to a flat where she is loved.

Dear ~~████~~ thought you would think this was funny –
the fold away bike has gone away! Would you believe
it someone actually stole that piece of crap from outside
the flat! I'm delighted means I don't have to worry
about getting it scrapped. Have learnt my lesson about
'cheap deals'... hope the thief is really pissed off
when they realise how crap the bike is!

See you later, ~~████~~

It can be difficult to resist a bargain. There is always that moment
of hope – that this time it won't be a trick or a scam, that you
will get a free lunch, it really was owned by one careful, old lady
driver, etc, etc. This note has all the hallmarks of someone still
naively hoping. It is rare that a theft can bring such joy. In this
case, not only has the theft got rid of the bike but it has also taken
away the physical reminder that the bike buyer had fallen for a
cheap deal again.

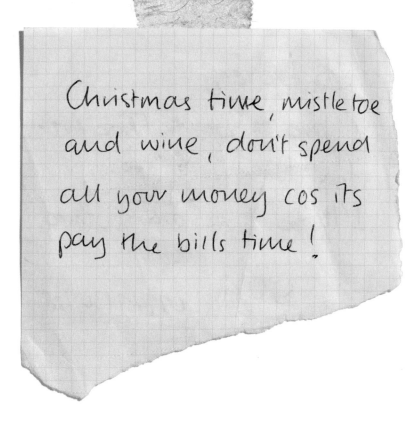

Christmas time, mistletoe and wine, don't spend all your money cos its pay the bills time!

Knowing the lyrics to a Cliff Richard song is bad enough but then using it to remind flatmates that even at Christmas they still have bills to pay, and therefore can't really go out and enjoy themselves, seems a little harsh.

Thank you for the money for the gas bill. Unfortunately you took so long to pay that the next one is now due. Will work out the totals when I get back in from work but have your cheque book at the ready. Cheers.

After several comments, dropped hints and notes, what are you meant to do when you cannot get your dues from someone? Short of getting the small claims courts involved, it can be almost impossible. The frustration in this note is palpable; you have eventually made some progress only to have to go through the whole rigmarole again. It is made even more annoying when you know they are trying to wear you down so eventually you will say, 'Oh forget it, I'll pay'. The 'being totally useless technique', as I have named it, is clever. It can save you a lot of money if you live with someone organised who will work out bills, cannot cope with red reminders and is not happy to live in debt. However, as you'll see later, such organised people can also be the type most likely to be a cleaning Nazi.

I found a little pile of toenails on my magazine. Could you not put your cheesy feet on my Vogue magazine, and unless you are collecting these nails as some sort of installation, could you throw them out, Margaret

These two sound like complete opposites. How ironic that the fashion bible should be strewn with toenails and smelling of 'cheesy feet'. The word 'installation' in the note leads me to guess the toenail clipper is an artist and for this reason they were very aware of the irony of the placement of their clippings and that, yes, this was a piece of art, a commentary on what they thought of fashion – cheesy.

STOP BUTT FLICKING INTO MY GARDEN!!!
YOUR NEIGHBOUR

I had to read this note a few times to get to grips with what was going on. Initially it sounded like some grizzly sex game I had not heard of. I thought there might be groups of people at twilight hanging their rears over garden fences while anonymous neighbours flicked their butts with garden utensils. It quickly became apparent that it was the equally antisocial habit of stubbing out a cigarette only to deposit it in the garden next door. This is often the result of out-of-window illicit smoking – a habit not just reserved for teens experimenting with the evil tobacco weed but of grown adults, who to get accepted into a flat have lied to the landlord that they are non-smokers. Similar lies are that they won't have people over to stay and they will not play loud music. Yeah, yeah, you lying butt flickers.

Hi lovely, I feel really bad for — — saying this and your brother is really lovely and I know he's at a bit of a loose end but how long is he going to be staying in our living room? It is beginning to get a bit awkward, and I don't see him making a big effort to get a job or find somewhere else to live. If he could arrange something for the weekend. Sorry I know you will understand.

P.S He has eaten quit a lot of my stuff

I can't help wondering how lovely the brother really was. I had a flatmate who had a creepy male friend. I hated it when the friend would come and stay. He wore full cycling gear (ie tight Lycra) at all times though there seemed to be no sign of a bike. The tightness of the attire made me nervous. He had a slightly musty smell. Altogether, there was too much oddness and staring for my liking. I didn't have the courage to say, 'Your friend is hanging around like a bad smell wearing clingy Lycra and is a total weirdo.' Perhaps I should have.

COULD YOU
NOT CUT UP MY MAGAZINES I HAVE
HAD THEM FOR YEARS AND
SOME OF THEM ARE ACTUALLY
VERY COLLECTABLE

This book is testimony to the fact that I love collecting things and this is why my heart went out to this note writer. I also thought this one was interesting as just recently a work colleague had told me of a similar incident – the unceremonious destruction of something they loved. Magazines and comics seem to be a common collectible. This pastime is very therapeutic and there is nothing more satisfying than watching your collection grow. It can also be deeply personal and the reasons for keeping things are not always apparent. The very fact that magazines, newspapers and comics are so throwaway and easily dismissed is what makes them so desirable. You can spend years hunting down an edition that everyone has had and remembers but that nobody has kept. The saddest part about this note is that the damage is done and there is no going back – for diehards it has the same impact as smashing an antique into little pieces.

NUFF RESPECT
TO THE
JESUS.

FEEL THE JESUS.
FEEL HIM

This was a Christmas message to the household. It beats 'Season's greetings and a Happy New Year'.

You stink like a
big fat stinker

PERSONAL HYGIENE AND
OTHER NOTES FROM THE BATHROOM

According to one of the many weird and wonderful statistics revealed each day in the press, every one of us spends an average of three years on the toilet during our lifetime. Finding solace in the bathroom is nothing new. In different cultures and throughout history there have been long and elaborate rituals and traditions relating to cleaning and hygiene. From the Romans and bathing to the Chinese and massage, huge amounts of time and thought have been put into what I refer to here as 'bathroom behaviour'.

However, for some people nowadays, busy lives mean such rituals have been either condensed or completely eradicated from daily routines. The well-being of teeth, skin and orifices are left in the much cleaner hands of the gods. These individuals waft around blissfully unaware of their odour. The fact is, we all struggle to detect our own smell. Mortifyingly, this is because we are no longer sensitive to it but, unfortunately, that doesn't apply to the odour of stinking flatmates. It takes a brave and/or tactless flatmate to let someone know that every time they speak they are gassing them with their halitosis. At the same time, however, a trip to any local supermarket would reveal rows of shelves and an array of products dedicated to cleaning and hygiene.

This is where characters at the other extreme of the cleaning spectrum emerge. For every flatmate who is cleaning averse, there is an almost uncanny tendency for there to be another who spends hours navel-gazing in the bath, while queues of grumpy cohabitants gather outside the locked bathroom waiting for this cleaning obsessive to finish preening.

I would like to believe there is some pay-off, however, for those who tend to find themselves on the outside of the locked bathroom door, as the character who takes up semi-residence in the bathroom is perhaps more likely to spend hours bleaching toilets and cleaning dishes. Flat-sharing is all about compromise, and so maybe those wasted minutes waiting each morning are levelled out by the time saved not doing the washing up that the cleaning obsessive gleefully takes care of. You may resent their bossiness and the smugness with which they tell you how much they clean the flat, but you can reply about being made to wait each day and, hey, you've avoided having to don the Marigolds.

Of course, if this ideal symmetry does not exist in your household, and the bathroom-hogger is only interested in cleaning themselves and not the communal areas of the flat, then it's time to start shamelessly banging on the bathroom door and drawing up time slots and chore sheets. It's amazing how often flatmates are forced to resort to these military-like forms to prevent otherwise sensible, mature people from causing grievous bodily harm.

So, bathroom hygiene is no laughing matter. It was recently reported that a man in Texas was stabbed at a bar for apparently not washing his hands. Just another example that germs are fatal and worth writing a note or two about.

This note originates from a problem that had gone beyond a joke. The writer was a guy who reported that the woman whom he shared a flat with had particularly thick curly hair … She was a nice girl in every other aspect apart from her unfortunate bathroom habit. In fact, she was, apparently, a bit of a head-turner. However, her manky secret was that after taking a bath, she never checked to see if the drain was clear. To quote the writer directly: 'What came out of the plug hole was like rope and it was making me feel sick'. This note is clearly a cry for help.

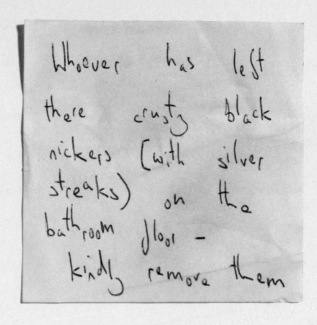

Whoever has left there crusty black nickers (with silver streaks) on the bathroom floor - kindly remove them

We all know what is being talked about (or written about) here, but we wish we didn't. While we all have biological functions, we generally don't want to think about them. The recipient of this note, however, had it thrust into her face by a person she had to see every day. Not physically thrust – God, that would be awful! When I spoke to the man who sent this, he expressed surprise that the girl whose knickers were being discussed cried when she got the note. There is only one word worse than the c-word: it is the other c-word – crusty.

Important:

Has anyone seen a William Hill betting slip. I think it was in the sitting room yesterday with a bunch of other receipts?

Sorry I ran out of bog roll

This note paints a very clear picture of this household and it isn't too good. They might not have bog roll in the toilet but I bet they have a few cans of lager in the fridge. It's a question of priorities, I suppose. Let's just hope the slip wasn't a winner.

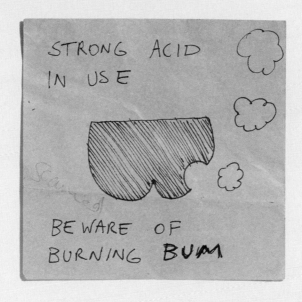

This note is considerate on many levels. Not only have they decided to clean the toilet with something so strong it could probably lift paint, they have written *and* illustrated a warning. This has got to be a dream flatmate, though one can only wonder why industrial-strength cleaning materials were necessary in the first place.

██████████

do not have you
washing machine on
at 2-45 Am
please?
my bedroom is just
underneath it.
Sometimes you machine
is on at midnight
but   2 45 am
it is too much
your sincerely

██████████

you suffering
neighbour
X

I was always under the illusion that if you use your appliances in your house at night it is cheaper. Where I found that nugget of information from, I am not sure, but I bet the person to whom this is addressed thinks the same. Perhaps, however, he is quite the opposite of frugal. It looks to me like after having a big night out, he regularly returns to the reality of no clean underpants for the morning. If there is one thing worse than a hangover, it is a hangover with dirty pants on.

WHAT IS THAT SMELL?!

Whoever thinks they may have any responsibility for the piss/wet dog smell out here could you please do something about it!! it's grim!

Communal areas in flats are often the focus of heated debates. Who buys the light bulbs? Who vacuums the hallway? Who takes responsibility for the bins? Who deals with the piss/wet-dog smell? Given the volume of people who go through these areas, it is understandable they may be a little, shall we say, aromatic.

You're patient, you try, you leave notes, drop subtle hints. Training some people to be aware of their surroundings can be a painstaking process. Many are oblivious to tasks that have to be done around the house to make it function and habitable for all concerned. A major issue is putting out rubbish for collection. It is amazing how difficult otherwise smart people find this. The scribe of this note has obviously worked tirelessly to get her fellow cohabiters to take part in this task and relieve herself of one of the household chores. So close and yet so far – the bag went out, but just the wrong one. This is a case of if you want it done, do it yourself. Or move.

YOU PROMISED + I QUOTE
"IF WE ALL BUY TOILET ROLLS,
WE WILL NEVER HAVE TO DO
IT AGAIN" (EMPHASIS WRITER'S)

WHAT DO YOU CALL THIS THEN?
THAT'S RIGHT! THE END OF
THE LAST ROLL.

CHEERS LIAR.

A favourite old chestnut of communal living and communal lies. Namely, that if flatmates all buy essentials whenever they go to the shops, the flat will not run out of stuff. Unfortunately, it is only the conscientious who do it and the non-conscientious who abuse it!

IF YOU ARE GOING TO PUT 'STUFF' DOWN THE TOILET (WAS THAT RICE PUDDING OR VOM OR WHAT?)... TOOK ME AGES TO UNCLOG IT, FUCKING DISGUSTING TO COME HOME TO!

6

Vomit is a difficult subject to bring up. Sorry. Gags aside (sorry again), it can be very awkward. And yet from my note collecting it seems to be a common anxiety. While it was always reassuring as a child to have your mum standing over you mopping your brow, holding back your hair as you threw up your dinner, when you find yourself in a flat of non-family members the last thing you want is an audience. Nearly as bad as finding yourself in this predicament is someone else finding the evidence. A shameful, hazy night is brought back with full force when someone refers to the bits of a doner kebab they have found floating in the pan. The rice pudding mentioned in this note is particularly interesting as there is no mention of the cubed carrot that we all know always appears in vomit regardless of what you have eaten.

Humour can often be a good way of broaching a difficult topic. Bodily odours not only fill a room but can also cling to everyone in that room. Before you know it, you all stink. But how do you address a grown adult who appears not to have worked out how to clean himself? It's difficult but occasionally the severity of the problem means action has to be taken. As an alternative to leaving deodorant out, this note is clear and to the point. Bravo!

you ok? heard you on
the big white telephone
all night, and a lot of
banging and crashing.
Going out for a full English,
but I am guessing you
won't be up for it.
See you later

'The big white telephone' – I have not heard this euphemism for a long time. The phrase I am accustomed to is a little more elaborate: on the big white telephone talking to Hughie and Ralph. It's slightly dated now, with more modern favourites such as 'a pavement pizza' taking over. I like this note as there is an undertone of Schadenfreude. The author must know the last thing the recipient would want at this stage is a full English. In fact, even the thought will probably have them rushing right back to the loo. Feigning concern, this note was a successful way of getting someone back for interrupting a good night's sleep.

This is one of the rare notes that I got an explanation with, and one that's not as confusing as it initially sounds. Being a raven-haired beauty, the young lady of the house had a lot of strapping chaps visiting her abode. These strong, fit men obviously ate a huge amount to maintain their bulk. Unfortunately, the creaking plumbing system had been installed in Victorian times, an era when everyone was shorter and narrower, and probably lived on a lump of coal and two peas a day, meaning their waste was minimal. As a result of several cloggings, it became apparent that when visiting this lady it was better to make sure you had done your 'big business' beforehand, unless you wanted to spend the rest of the time there with rubber gloves on and a plunger in hand.

Wednesday

Ev.

Been thinking about what you said about the boys in the house not pulling our weight, we would just like to point out that we don't use nearly as much toilet paper or house hold cleaning stuff as the girls — so i don't think we should have to split the costs.

ta. Steve

Have you been counting? You will now. That's right, counting the sheets – how many sheets of toilet paper you use on every visit. Are you a folder or a crumpler? In doing this book I have found out the most interesting and personal details about people: the lengths individuals will go to with loo roll, peeling apart the double ply, wrapping it around a finger (oh God, no). I have been informed that actually the healthiest way to go to the toilet is to squat as this straightens out the lower intestine and thus there should be less need for the paper. I have yet to find myself squatting on the edge of the loo seat, for I am happy to indulge myself and use toilet paper. Steve's argument may not be so outlandish as it might appear on first sight. When researching this topic it has only been men who have confessed to resorting to using, among other things, newspaper and other paperwork (see the betting-slip note earlier). Mind you, maybe women are just not as prepared to admit to it and, who knows, it could be a very efficient way of recycling 'glossy' magazines. Even better, it could be a sweet revenge on the face of some of our beloved celebrities in the gossip rags.

Your weak bladder is making me tired! When you go to the toilet – <u>please</u>, please <u>don't</u> flush – unless it is major! The plumbing and the pipes make such a noise next to my room – I keep getting woken up. SUE (aka tired and grumpy flatmate)

An important requirement of any decent flatmate in a flat with crumbling plumbing is a strong bladder. My father once told me about sneaking home after a night out as a student to be greeted by his rather angry mother. When asked how much he had had to drink, he said, 'About six pints.' 'Six pints? I couldn't drink six pints of water!' his mother answered. My father made the true and rather amusing observation that he didn't think he could drink six pints of water either. His mother didn't see the funny side and, unfortunately for him, it resulted in a stern ticking off. Now I have no idea about the strength of my father's bladder, but what is it about booze that you can just keep going? Ah, that's right, it's addictive! But the most interesting boozing phenomenon is that no matter how much you drink, you always seem to expel double the amount. This can be a tiring pursuit of getting up and blindly padding along hallways fumbling with door handles in a desperate search for the loo. I have heard many, sadly not apocryphal, stories of gents found peeing in cupboards, ashtrays and wardrobes. But as Steve pointed out in a previous note – at least that means they use less toilet paper. Every cloud.

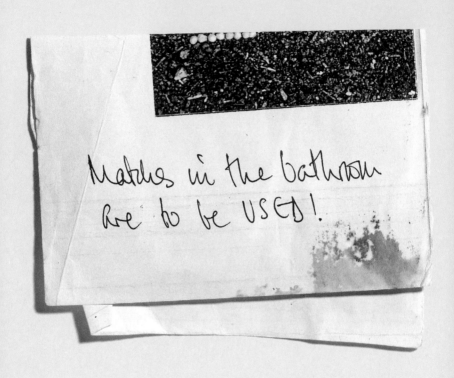

Matches in the bathroom are to be USED!

The original air freshener. Never mind your fancy pot pourris, candles or scented solvents; the good old-fashioned match is the best way of burning off any methane that is lingering in the air. Just be sure to keep it away from 'the biological methane valve' to avoid seriously unpleasant burns.

oh OK I get the hint playing RESPECT at top volume gave it away. I didn't mean to disrespect you by walking in to the bathroom, but you hadn't lock the door.

I have been inspired. Less confrontational (or more cowardly) than note writing is simply to play music to get your point across. Other possible tracks could be 'Welcome To The Monkey House' by the Dandy Warhols, or '[I Hate] Everything About You' by Ugly Kid Joe. Gosh, I feel a compilation CD coming. It gives a whole new meaning to 'house music'.

I HAVE HAD TO
CHUCK OUT YOUR HORRIBLE
OLD BLANKET — IT WAS FULL OF
MINGING MONTHS. I ONLY REALISED WHEN I WENT
TO GET MY BLACK DRESS FOR THE BALL ON SATURDAY TO
FIND SO MANY HOLES IT LOOKED LIKE LACE. YOU
ARE GOING TO HAVE TO CHUCK OUT LOADS OF YOUR
STUFF AS THEY HAVE GOT EVERYWHERE. APPARENTLY
IF YOU FREEZE SOME OF THE CLOTHES THEY ARE
RETRIEVABLE AS IT KILLS THE EGGS BUT I THINK
WE SHOULD JUST CHUCK EVERYTHING.

Some people are phobic of spiders, others birds, but for me it's moths. My first issue with them is their stupidity. Evolution has not been kind to moths. They fly around with no real purpose until they eventually die, their little corpses stuck in a lamp or, worse, in a cloth while the cleaning obsessive is hard at work. When they are alive, they are ugly, always beige and have a creepy, macabre dust covering their wings. But the thing that really makes me detest these small and, I have to admit, relatively harmless insects is their diet. Why, oh why, do they find natural fibre so nutritious? Surely if there was any kind of sustenance in non-synthetics we would all be munching our woolly jumpers? It is amazing the amount of damage such small creatures can do. They can destroy whole wardrobes of clothes, and procreate as if they are actually important in our ecosystem. As the note mentions, getting rid of them is almost impossible. The only real solution is to use mothballs, which could be re-termed living creature balls, as their distinctive smell would repel anyone or anything. Whichever way you look at it, once the moths decide to hang out in your wardrobe, it's time to move.

Ha ha I have just worked out why
there is a Ragu jar lid sitting out
with some water in it .... a very
inventive way of preserving your
contact when you come home a bit
worse for wear

I always wanted to wear glasses as a child. I thought it would make me look well read and grown up. As the youngest of the family, I thought my siblings would suddenly sit up and listen to my inspired nuggets of information if I had some facial accessories to hide behind. As an adult, I now pray the inevitable specs will be a few years off as I see the hassle they cause. Contacts have a whole array of issues associated with them: grit, drying out, and slipping behind your eye into your brain. Soft, hard or simply lost contacts might look good, but they can be a real trauma. So after a long day and an even longer night out, it is understandable that having to fiddle around with fluids and small containers, which is not that easy when sober, is not as appealing as simply collapsing into bed. Yet is it worth that extra hour indeed if it means having your lenses welded to your eyes in the morning? So this note offers the perfect solution. It is very straightforward: grab the nearest container, in this case a spaghetti-sauce jar lid, fill lid with some bog standard water and decant lenses into the water. Result: useless contact lenses no doubt coated in several billion bacteria. Still, better out than in.

I read an article not so long ago that reported that Madonna allegedly said (I repeat, allegedly) on a TV show that peeing in the shower is good for you. Apparently, it acts as an antiseptic and the enzymes fight off things such as athlete's foot. I have always been a little uneasy about celebrity-endorsed theories since Doctor Atkins died. Pass the carb-packed sandwich, I'm off to buy some bleach!

ASHTRAY NEXT TO
THE BATH — You CAN
TELL WHICH IS WHICH
BY THE SIZE
Signed
X
(THE ONE WHO USES THE BATH)

This seems very Hugh Hefner – smoking in the bath. I would
have thought the logistics of this are quite tricky. Unless you
have your very own playgirl bunnies to hold your, er, cigar, in
the bath, would it not be going out all the time? It's hard enough
finding the soap in the bath never mind a lighter and a pack of
twenty cigarettes. Probably better just to quit.

If you saw me
running across the
hall this morning I
was not, as you probably
think naked, I was just
wearing hairy pants...honest!!!
hmm very embarrassed,
was a bit drunk and
confused

My parents grew up in the 1940s and recount horror stories of swimming lessons at local public baths. Besides no heating, caustic soap, and corn plasters in the pool, the worst thing they told me about was swimsuits you could rent! If the thought of sharing these garments is not grim enough, just consider for a moment what they were made of. I am told that before the days of figure-hugging Spandex and Lycra, bathing suits were more of the woollen kind – eugh, itchy. I can't help thinking of these bathing suits when I read this note. I wouldn't have believed in this attire if I hadn't seen a stand-up routine by Billy Connolly where he also talks about these very garments and the way they became like a dead weight, sagging from your body like a big damp coat as you entered the water. From now on, I am going to swim naked and say I am wearing my brown-mohair bikini bottoms. You have been warned.

I didn't realise you were so musical, I can hear you bum trumpeting all night!

There is not much you can do about noisy innards. To hear someone else's 'bum trumpeting' all night may be irritating, but there is not a lot the player can do bar stuffing a cork up their — well, you get the idea. Trying to hold wind in can be very uncomfortable and result in weird internal noises. Everyone knows what it really is, so you might as well let it out. And at night you don't have these forms of control anyway. One solution could be removing certain foods such as beans and sprouts from the offending flatmate's cupboard space, thereby subtly changing their diet. I know of one flat of weight-conscious girls who suffered at the hands of rice cakes. One young lady described the side effects of eating the offending article as 'a thousand mini explosions in your stomach'. Good God. The healthier the foodstuff, the more of a reaction it has on one's digestion. It is for this reason I have decided I do not want to meet or live with any glamorous film stars. I suspect they have mouths like sewers and smell of farts. That's the real reason Marilyn's skirt used to fly up. *Phewwww!*

Danielle,

Called the landlord about the hot water. He says it won't be fixed for <u>at least</u> another week. Not a lot we can do about it. At least, we are getting fit by going to the gym all the time to use the showers! See you later, gorgeous. xoxo

This is not that uncommon. I have heard of people living in studios where there is no running water, cooking or washing facilities. As a result you do a lot of visiting friends, going to the public baths and drinking the free milk in Starbucks. I know of one landlord who jovially tried to deal with the broken-boiler situation by joking that his tenants' waterless, gym-going existence might make them suitable for SAS training or for going on some sort of bush-tucker trail in the Australian outback. What a fucker.

Could somebody explain why my door has magically come off its hinges and is lying in the middle of my room?

Very pissed off, can't even bloody get dressed or changed.

Gabs.

When this note was passed to me, it was obvious the writer was still 'very pissed off'. I began to understand her emotional state when she elaborated further. The door had been a bit on the wobbly side as it was an old flat with old doors. She suspected a flatmate had pushed at it to get into her room and borrow her hairdryer, and had used such force that the door, which was not very stable in the first place, came right off its hinges and hey, *timber*! Things were made worse by the fact it was very heavy and, en route to the floor, put a huge dent in her table and smashed some small ornaments to obliteration. Nice.

I really enjoyed the party
but ~~haven't~~ enjoyed been
the one left to tidy up.
ESPECIALLY as I found
a soiled pair of y fronts
behind the cistern. who
the hell was that, thought
I was going to be sick,

you each owe me at least
a pint.

Sometimes a party can be just that bit *too* exciting. It puts a lot of pressure on your body: copious amounts of liquid, probably dodgy food, smoking like a beagle and the increasingly common drug-induced runs. There is probably nothing worse. You take a mood-enhancing something or other and suddenly it all seems great; you're floating, and you're the life and soul, dancing like you're fluid, being as funny and witty as Oscar Wilde. And then it happens. You feel everything in your stomach move down a notch or two and the curry you had a couple of hours ago is now resting like lead and wants out. You look over and, as with all good parties, there is a huge queue outside the toilets mostly made up of pretty girls in twos. Blatantly, they are all going to be some time as they get themselves as addled on some substance as you are. By the time you eventually reach the almost mythical toilet, you can hardly dance your fingers down your flies quick enough before a deep and putrid, not to mention loud, mass evacuates your body, soiling your pants in the process. You come out of the loo, head hung as young pretty girls' dilated eyes widen at the stench following you. Or you could just hide your Y-fronts behind the cistern. Sorted!

Dear All,

I have noticed that my shampoo seems to be very diluted. Kindly do not use it and then try and deceive me by adding, what I can only hope is water - OK? Karen

126

I have heard of people topping up miniatures of vodka in mini bars at hotels with water, but shampoo? That is truly cheap. The added element of hope in this note panics me, especially after having read a report of a man who was caught peeing in his work colleagues' communal coffee machine. I too can only hope that Karen has been washing her hair with a water/shampoo combination. Liquids such as beer are apparently good for your coiffure, but urine I have yet to see as a crucial new ingredient in one of those complicated shampoo adverts from 'laboratories herbal hair defineutraline' or the likes. Bet Karen's hair looks great but smells like — well, like she didn't just step out of a salon.

Two things, could you stop leaving plates & coffee mugs in the bathroom, second thing I do not think it is a very good idea to eat and drink while on the loo!

I wonder if anyone has rented out their bathroom? It has all the necessary amenities, such as running water and a place to sleep, although not really anything for cooking, unless you are happy to turn on the shower and steam your food.

I lick my cheese

FOOD AND OTHER NOTES FROM THE KITCHEN

Everyone knows the best place to be at a party is the kitchen. The party drugs of our generation are in our food. Have a swig of one of the many neon fizzy drinks now available over the counter or chow down on a packet of sweets and before you know it you're as high as a kite. Some of the most creative notes have been written by individuals high on E numbers, not E.

Artificial additives, colours and preservatives aside, the kitchen can produce sensory overload and, no matter how many rotas you write, there is always the potential for disagreement. We all think we have the best taste, but one man's meal is another's leftovers. And the way and what we eat is very personal and can structure a day, so people can be very protective about their food. It's a primal instinct. Needless to say, vegetarians, vegans, those who are lactose intolerant and old-school junk-eaters do not survive well in the same house.

Many of these note writers are on a diet. If you are on a diet, everyone is affected. If you have ever included mung beans into your five portions of fruit and veg a day, you will be aware of the amazing chemical reactions they induce in the stomach. Gaseous, grumpy and minus two hundred calories, the 'dieter' comes home to find the kitchen in disarray. It takes a strong character to resist leaving a note, or even eating the notepad. The lady on the telly who examines your poo and the man who makes juices both have a lot to answer for. I would like to know how many households have been woken by the dulcet tones of a smoothie machine pulsing away at 6.30am before a detoxifying run. Mind you, it's not just the dieters that are smelly. Have you ever opened a pack of wafer-thin turkey? It smells like farts. Why? But frankly who cares – it serves you right for purchasing something described as '80% meat' (what the hell is the other 20%?). Even worse is mechanically retrieved meat – no human could bring themselves to retrieve it without gagging, but we are expected to munch enthusiastically on it.

At the other end of the scale is the 'foodie' – those who know their chard from their kale. Pretensions aside, they are actually just greedy. They like gorging. Mind you, it isn't the greedies, sorry, foodies, who are suffering from the recent obesity problems. The foodies are at least eating products that have some vague resemblance to food. The food they eat hasn't been shaped into a rectangle or a hilarious twizzle shape. No, the people who are getting fat beyond the supermarkets' wildest dreams are the TV-dinner diners.

The TV-dinner diners do not spend long periods of time in the kitchen, as there is no preparation involved with their food – apart from unwelding plastic food from a plastic container. Everything has already been done for them and, in their flats, the busiest door is that of the freezer. In fact, you could be forgiven for mistaking their behind for their face, as the only thing you ever see of them is their arse hanging out of the freezer while they forage for more frozen foods.

Whether it is a case of too much or too little, food can be an obsession and so it is a fertile ground for note writing. If you are addicted to anything, having it or depriving yourself of it can send you over the edge.

ARE YOU *TRYING TO
GROW PENICILLIN IN THIS
COFFEE MUG. COULD YOU CLEAN
IT US PLEASE 'COS IT'S
MINGING. THANKS Kx.

We have a future chemist on our hands. We should encourage this kind of DIY chemistry. Penicillin was in fact found by growing mould on bread by, eh well, let's see, oh yes! Mr Penicillin, so this young grunge may have the cure for cancer festering in the bottom of his cup. On a more sinister side, the spores that could be exploding out of the cup can lead to all sorts of problems, including breathing difficulties. So, no, it's not the forty cigarettes you're smoking that is destroying your lungs but possibly the washing up!

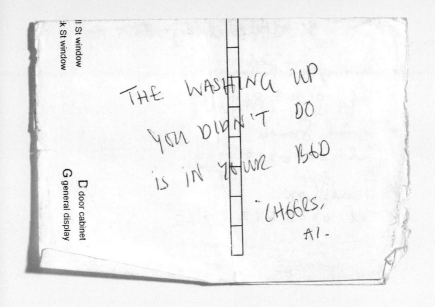

THE WASHING UP
YOU DIDN'T DO
IS IN YOUR BED
·· CHEERS,
AL -

ll St window
k St window

D door cabinet
G general display

If you have ever lived with someone who has lower hygiene standards than yourself, this note will appeal to you. While researching this book, I found out that there are a range of tips that have become almost folklore for tackling difficult cohabiting issues. Putting washing up in the bed of a non-washer-upper is one of these tips. From where these tips originate I do not know – they must be passed from generation to generation, or maybe there are groups of very clean people meeting to discuss tried and tested techniques. I have been told about the washing-up-in-the-bed technique several times. Trying to guilt trip the non-washer-upper into doing the task just doesn't work – they don't care. My tip is: use paper plates. Failing that, resort to the technique employed by one particularly scanky individual who lived with a friend – he covered dirty plates with tin foil before depositing his nightly takeaway onto them.

Please don't soak my stuff that's made out of wood — it bends + cracks them when the fibres get full of water

cheers!

Cheers indeed! But this was both written and received with a sense of desperation. This person was so pedantic that every day there was a new message. It got to the point where the flatmates dreaded coming home or waking up as there would be another little scrap of paper waiting for them. The worst thing was that you often didn't even know what you had done ...

Touché! Strangely I have heard of this kind of behaviour before. Very primitive – like marking your territory. It works. I wouldn't go near this fridge even if my life depended on it.

PLEASE DONT TURN THIS INTO AN ARGUMENT
AS IT NEEDNT BE
IF WE CAN BE MATURE ABOUT THIS

IT WOULD BE RIDICULOUS FOR EACH
OF US TO HAVE TO LABEL ALL OUR
BELONGINGS IN THE FLAT

ALL IAM ASKING IS THAT WHEN YOUR
BOYFRIEND FINDS SOMETHING HE WANTS
TO THROW AWAY BUT DOESNT BELONG
TO HIM

HE ASKS THE PERSON WHO OWNS IT FIRST

WE CAN AVOID ANY UNPLEASANT FEELING
IN THE FLAT IF WE JUST OBSERVE
COMMON COURTESY, AND WE ALL
WANT TO LIVE IN A FLAT THAT HAS
A GOOD FEELING ABOUT IT

I. AM SURE YOU CAN UNDERSTAND THIS
FROM MY POINT OF VIEW, AND WE CAN
SORT THIS OUT POLITELY

HAVE A GOOD EASTER

'We can be mature about this', or 'I don't want this to be a big problem' etc, is generally to be reread as 'this is going to be a huge problem'. To be compelled to commit it to paper rather than muttering it under your breath on your own means you can't be mature about it. It *is* going to be an argument and you are *not* sorry about it.

Glad to see some weight issues are being addressed with this clever, modern-day twist on a traditional nursery rhyme. This may be the way forward in treating childhood obesity – simply by changing words and lyrics such as: *Jack and Jill went for the burn up a hill.*

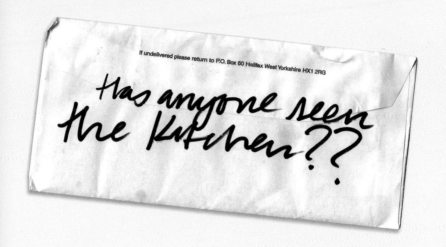

If undelivered please return to P.O. Box 60 Halifax West Yorkshire HX1 2RG

Has anyone seen the Kitchen??

This is a work of genius. Funny, short and to the point, it sums up what appears to be a scenario full of despair. It evokes those horrible feelings of panic and irritation when you misplace keys and wallets. I think a very apt reply to this note would be: can you remember where you last saw it? Anyway, it sounds as though this kitchen isn't so much used as abused. It conjures up images of neon-orange-sweet'n'sour-sauce-stained worktops. Weeks of ungluing noodles from plates will ensue.

ADAM

GOOD LUCK TONIGHT,
I have left everything
out for you with
INSTRUCTIONS so should be
fine — remember To lower
the FROZEN PEAS slowly
INTO the boiling WATER
So you don't splash
                yourself!

                        CLAIRE

P.S remember
To switch the oven off.

There is a fine line between being helpful and coming across like a control freak. I think Claire might have crossed that line.

I needed that
ham!
Really needed
it.

GO SHOPPING

There is an explanation with this note. The recipient said the
writer was convinced other flatmates were stealing her food
which is understandably annoying, especially if you 'really need
it'. (Was she basing a whole meal round a slice of ham?) The
reality, however, according to my source, was rather different.
Apparently, nothing had been taken, especially as the other
flatmates were both vegetarian. A ham paranoia had set in.
Not only had vegetarians stolen her ham, but they had stolen
it when she *really* needed it. It had been a Ham Emergency.

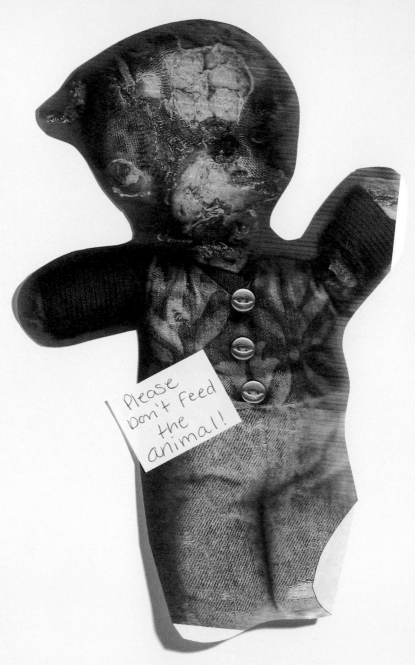

They say the difference between humans and animals is that humans have a conscience. Living together sometimes suggests otherwise. Flatmates may take on a human shape, but their habits, especially eating habits, sometimes suggest they are closer to a feral creature than a human. I have visions of frightened flatmates slipping wafer-thin turkey under this person's door rather than risk unleashing him on the rest of the flat. In fact, he probably hasn't come out of his room all winter, preferring to survive on the small morsels of food caught in his beard.

This is my.
Breakfast.
I wouldn't look
it looks like a
dogs bottom!

I am informed that the breakfast in question was a bran, muesli and cranberry-based concoction. Good for the body, but not so pleasant on the eye. The note is worryingly descriptive, but a cunning way to put people off stealing the cereal. Trying to follow a diet in a flat is always going to be difficult. There is temptation everywhere. You might have stocked up on quinoa, but if your flatmate has family packs of crisps and chocolate the draw can be too much. Then there's the preparation. If your kitchen is the same size as a shower cubicle, monopolising the kitchen while you chop three kilograms of vegetables every morning will not make you very popular, no matter how much weight you lose or how healthy you become. What's wrong with toast? It's a good-size portion, quick to make, healthy, and generally doesn't look like a dog's bottom.

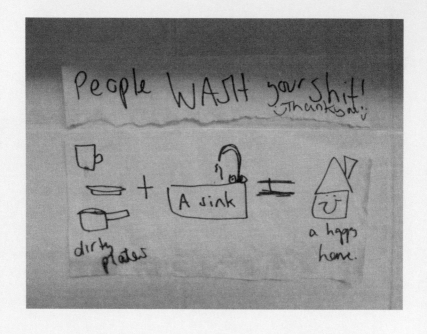

It might not be particularly eloquent, but you can definitely feel the anger in this note. I am not quite sure what the 'shit' refers to, but I can only guess and hope from the illustration that it means washing up, as this tends to be one of the main sources of argument in shared accommodation. There seems to be a little back-pedalling with the venom, as there is a slightly meek 'thank you' added at the end, though that could just be sarcasm.

I love this inventive use of an advertising slogan here. OK, so they might not have any fat left to coat their toast, but at least they still have their sense of humour.

House of fun members!
Please can we start a new policy of after every cup of tea, after breakfast etc
washing up after ourselves all the time
instead of leaving everything for the dinner-
time wash. It's unfair, because invariably
one person ends up washing dishes all
the time AND it's also bloody unhygienic
as dishes sit there, sometimes overnight,
and are disgusting & difficult to clean
when someone finally decides to clean
up.
I'm sorry to be an anal-mum, but
please, it's the one thing that really
bothers me.
Cheers

House of Fun? House of Fun? The irony! I don't think there is much fun going on in this house. In fact, I suspect mere breathing might annoy this House of Pedantry member. More often than not, notes such as these contain lots of apologies about bringing the issue to attention. You know, the type that begin with: 'I'm embarrassed to mention this, but …', 'I can't believe I'm writing this, but …', 'I never thought I'd see the day when it would be necessary to write a note like this, but …', or 'I'm a complete a**hole which is why I'm writing and not talking to you, but …' (well, maybe ignore the last one). The point is, these are empty apologies as the writer clearly still feels compelled to write the note and doesn't seem to have realised that the awkwardness a note can cause is worse than the problem written about in the first place. Also, check out the use of the word 'policy', which sounds more like the Houses of Parliament than a House of Fun …

Hi Guys,

Have been WORKING
on one of MY CAKE
recipies this after
NOON, would love to
hear your OPINION
on how to make it really
scrummy. Help
yourself, AND tell me
what you think...
NOT enough Ginger?

Making cakes? Scrummy? Enough ginger? I imagine this is the kind of note Nigella Lawson once wrote to her flatmates. It seems to come from another age, when people drank ginger beer and went punting on the lake instead of snorting suspicious powders before an evening of dogging. Scrummy!

I know that in the morning it is much easier to make your scrambled eggs in the microwave or that it means there are no pans to wash. But this morning I realised there was something in my tea -- there was scrambled egg stuck in the bottom of my mug! DONT use the mugs as the egg welds itself to it or gives me a very nasty surprise in the morning. Use the bowls or just the bloody pan. A.

Often when I am reading these notes, I can't help feeling there must be more important issues in the world to care about. Missing ham, licked cheese – they're hardly international crises. But I can understand why the writer lost her sense of humour here. The last thing you need when you stumble down to the kitchen in the morning, half-asleep, is to be confronted with a strange fungus-like object in the bottom of your tea mug. People's stomachs aren't at their strongest at that hour and a new type of tea-flavoured egg-nog is not going to help matters.

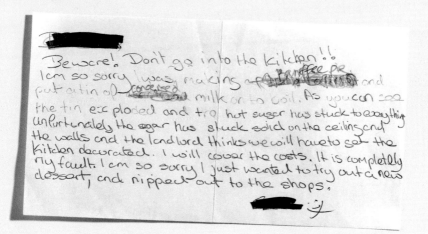

Beware!. Don't go into the kitchen!!.
I am so sorry I was making ~~toffee pr~~ and
put a tin of ~~condensed~~ milk on to boil. As you can see
the tin exploded and the hot sugar has stuck to everything
Unfortunately the sugar has stuck solid on the ceiling and
the walls and the landlord thinks we will have to get the
kitchen decorated. I will cover the costs. It is completely
my fault. I am so sorry I just wanted to try out a new
dessert, and nipped out to the shops.

I have always been a little anxious about dying a comical death. Being consumed by hot, sticky condensed milk is a death that is, yes, wait for it, bitter-sweet. This note points out how dangerous (and expensive) this situation could be. I just can't help thinking this would be a fitting death for Delia.

YOU MIGHT BE
WONDERING WHAT THAT
HORRENDOUS SMELL
THROUGHOUT THE
WHOLE FLAT IS.
DO YOU REMEMBER BEFORE
YOU WENT OUT YOU PUT
SOME EGGS ON TO THE
BOIL? OBVIOUSLY NOT!
AS AFTER WHAT HAD
BEEN 7 HOURS ON
THE BOIL THEY
NATURALLY EXPLODED!!!!

I HAD TO NOT ONLY
CLEAN UP THE MESS, BUT
ALSO PUT UP WITH THAT
STINK ALL NIGHT. SORT
YOURSELF OUT - COULD HAVE
BEEN REALLY FUCKING
DANGEROUS. I KNOW
YOU HAVE GOT A LOT
ON YOUR MIND BUT
THERE ARE OTHER
PEOPLE LIVING HERE.

I have every sympathy for the recipient of this note as I once did something very similar. Eggs can create bad smells. So can burnt-out pans. Exploding blackened eggs in burnt-out pans raise the bar however to a whole new level. What is behind this kind of disaster? If you have a mind full of ideas, some things can easily be categorised as unimportant. As soon as the practical things you should be remembering re-enter your head, they are almost immediately eradicated to make room for the huge, amazing and monumental new genius thoughts you are growing. I like to think Einstein was always putting eggs on to boil and forgetting about them.

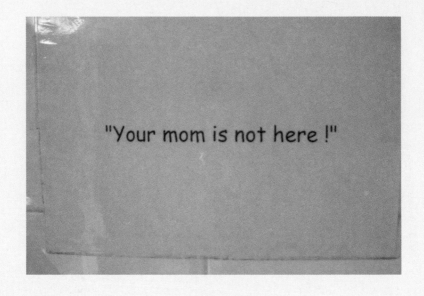

Mom may not be here, but someone has gone to a lot of trouble to have this note printed and laminated. This is taking note writing to a new and, to my mind, scarily professional level. What next? A flashing-dot matrix sign? Billboards?

Thank you for
Making my tea this
Morning I am Just
too tired to talk

Early morning is often when notes come into play. Slowly, the ability to speak comes back just enough to allow you to make barely audible grunts and gestures in the direction of sustenance. I think this note would be great if it was sold as one of a set of flash cards that could just be held up in the morning saying: 'Please', 'Thank you', 'Where's the milk?', 'I hate you', etc.

Could you STOP
chewing my pens
and pencils?
They are quite
expensive as
they are proper
drawing ones....
maybe you should
have a bigger
lunch!

This is a nasty habit. You never know where a pen or pencil has
been. I hazard a guess in someone's hand, and that alone is
enough to make you stop chewing.

This note stands alone. Too funny to argue with.

Too much
coffee —
apologise !
think that is shy
I am being
particularly
hostile.

One of the most common worldwide addictions is to caffeine. For a long time it has had a very negative press and been viewed as a vice, but recently it is becoming more and more apparent that caffeine isn't all bad; in fact, caffeine is pretty cool. For example, results of research conducted in Osaka University in Japan contained the finding that 'people who drink coffee every day could lower their risk of diabetes by 33%'.

It's not all just about lattes and skinny mochas, however. My favourite caffeine product is a pair of stockings available on the Internet that contain caffeine 'micro capsules' which are activated by body heat. (They stimulate cells and burn fat before you ask.) I guess anything is worth a try. I fear that an addictive drug being administered through clothing into your skin would have a great black-market value.

This note is especially interesting as the writer knows they are hostile but just can't stop drinking coffee – this is a true addict. I wonder if they were wearing the stockings at the time to get a double shot?

I think I should point out to who ever has been eating the stuff in the fridge with the foil over it, it is actually raw sausage meat that i was going to use as stuffing. It hasn't been cooked yet so will probably make you very ill. Guess you have learnt your lesson by eating other peoples stuff!

If you have ever had any form of food poisoning, you will be feeling the bile gathering at the back of your throat as you read this. I like to think of this person in a dark kitchen, the only light coming from the open fridge that they are squatting in front of. They scoop small balls of the soft, moist substance into their mouth with their fingers. Suddenly, they notice a note. They stop their gorging, removing their hand from under the foil, careful not to make a noise. Their eyes frantically scan down the note, locking on the word 'raw'. They feel a horrible sensation. Not only have they been 'caught' with their hands in someone else's food, but it has just dawned on them that a ball of raw flesh is swilling around their stomach. Cold sweats, groaning noises from all orifices; this is more than a lesson. This is a brutal, possibly fatal punishment. I pray this person was under the influence of alcohol when they went on this feeding frenzy. Hopefully, the drink would numb the pain of the following few days stuck in the bathroom, head in their hands and dignity in the pan.

Someone
ate my Pasta!
I'm hungry.

A cry for help, and God knows, we have all been there. This is a sorrowful state of affairs that can drive any sane person over the edge: the end of the working day is approaching and you have mentally envisaged what you have in your share of the cupboard. In your head, you have put the ingredients together and come up with a genius plan for dinner. By the time you are on the bus up the road from work, you have virtually tasted the sumptuous dinner you are about to prepare. At no point has this involved having to make a last-minute trip to the corner shop to buy a heavily overpriced ingredient. But in a moment the crimson mist of 'stolen-ingredient rage' is about to descend. You get into the flat, take off your coat and kick off your shoes. You put a pan on the hob and reach into the cupboard only to grasp at thin air. A noise from the pit of your guts emerges: *What f*cker has taken my penne?*' There then follows a situation where you find yourself either chewing through a pot of pesto, or resigning yourself to standing in a lengthy queue of grumpy people to buy pasta for about forty-five quid at your local corner shop generally called 'Cost cutting' or something equally ironic without meaning to be. A 500% mark up. Nice.

EVERYDAY SHOPPING LIST.

1) Beer
2) Beer
3) More Beer
4) ciggies

any money left

5) wine for the odd balls

I sometimes think it would be humiliating if people knew what music I had on my iPod. I happily listen to one-hit wonders from the eighties and MOR pop, bobbing along pretending that I am actually listening to something from a small independent record label that is terribly highbrow and definitely not Busted.

It is for this reason I like this shopping list. The shopping list I would write down contains lots of words such as 'sundried', 'mulled' and 'organic'. The one in my head contains the words 'processed', 'full fat' and 'fun-size'. I admire the honesty in this note. All they really want is beer and fags, and no other rubbish.

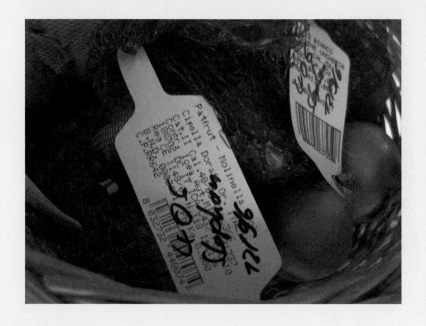

In this picture, 'Stephen' has put his name on all his onions. Stephen, they are onions. To the best of my knowledge, there is no shortage of onions and in the event you suddenly ran out of them all in one go, unless you live in the Orkneys, I do not believe you could not gain access to onions. Expensive cheese, a nobby bottle of wine, organic jam maybe – these are items perhaps worthy of marking, but onions?

I've looked all over the flat for it, not just in the kitchen, and I can't find my old porcelain teapot. I mean, who would steal a teapot, and what would they want with it?

A good rhetorical question. Who *would* steal a teapot from a flat, apart from a kleptomaniac? It is not the first object one would think of stealing. The sad truth of this note is that nobody stole the teapot – its disappearance was less of a kidnapping than a murder. No theft was involved; this note is about the death of a teapot. Perhaps accidentally nudged off the kitchen table, I suspect the remains were hidden by the culprit under a lot of rubbish and disposed of quickly, in the hope it would never be mentioned again.

Good grief, it sounds like this warning is too late. What horrible accident has happened with plastic near or on the appliance? I am going to have nightmares about molten bread bags wrapping themselves around faces leaving individuals writhing around their kitchen floor, when all they wanted was a slice of toast for their breakfast. This is the type of warning that made me cry as a child. Others were: 'Don't swallow chewing gum, it will wrap round your heart' and, 'Don't go near a food blender if you have long hair, it will get trapped in the mixers and your hair will be ripped off your head'. Suddenly, the kitchen is a terrifying place to venture into. I suspect this scaremongering comes from someone with a background in Health and Safety. Does this household have rope ladders for quick window exits, and do they practise evacuations in case of nuclear war? I mock, but I have just spat out my chewing gum and done a quick check of the windows in my flat.

I am really upset and confused. I take great joy and satisfaction in separating out the rubbish into the recycling bins that I have marked in the kitchen. I have labelled them and colour coded them to make it easier to know which bin to put glass plastic paper in etc So I was very angry to see that someone had obviously moved some of the rubbish around. I know this is MY quiche box that I put in the paper bin was in the glass bin. Are you sabotaging my recycling ??

C.

OK, OK, deriving this much joy from recycling sounds a little seventies but maybe this damn hippy has a point. Green issues have been volleyed about in the political arena for a few decades. Brought up as a last-minute topic – 'Oh, by the way the world is heating up 'n' stuff' – they have been treated in the same way as going to the dentist. Everyone knows that they really should go to the dentist regularly but they always leave it too late, going for an appointment only when an abscess rivalling the size of a human head has appeared. With the environment, the warnings are there; all the aches and pains of the earth are beginning to show, but not until the whole of Great Britain has been immersed in water will we really take the issues seriously. Until then, it is lone eco-warriors who will struggle to make the difference against all odds. Although this note makes me want to slap the writer with their quiche-eating, recycling ways, I know they are right.

What is it with onions? I did not know they were such a scarce resource or that they were the subject of so much discussion. Or is it a warning, like 'Sharks in water'? Is there an onion-phobic flatmate in the house?

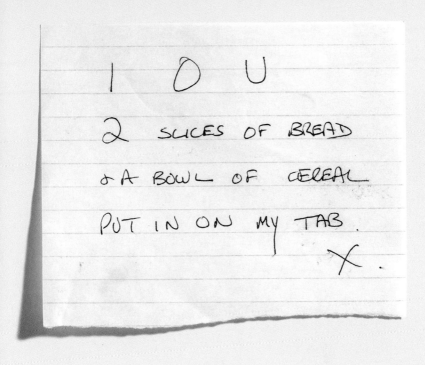

This note is like an old-fashioned bartering system. I used to swap two ends of a loaf for one decent slice with my flatmate. Twenty-five pence, I hear, is still the going rate for a single cigarette. Replacing food is almost not worthwhile; you are bound to get caught out. I heard of someone trying to replace milk by pouring more into the depleted carton, only to be caught out when the milk curdled. Unfortunately, this was discovered when the original milk owner had a big gulp of their soured tea. I think it's best to come clean or keep a tab.

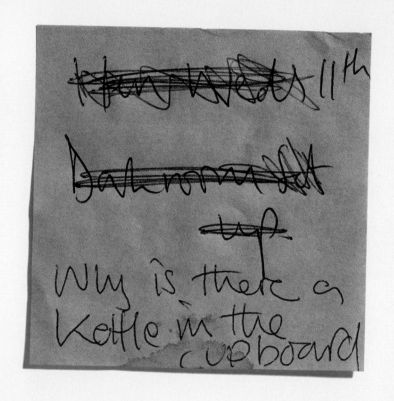

180

The background to this note is very interesting and a condition that I am sure has a scientific term – something like Domestic Stress Amnesia. The young lady who received this note said she had been doing a lot of revising for her finals. Her brain was pretty crushed with information and she had been living on adrenalin, nicotine and the ubiquitous caffeine. In her exhausted state she left her room and went to the kitchen to make her four-hundredth (approximately) cup of tea. In her preoccupation with holding the thoughts and facts she had just learnt in her head, she put the tea cup down where the kettle usually sat and put the kettle in the cupboard before returning to her room. A few hours later, she came down for another tea break to find this note. It was only at this point she realised that she was maybe overdoing the studying and decided to have a rest before she lit her hair and washed a cigarette.

leaving photocopies of
parts of the bible round
the kitchen and
stuck up on the fridge
is not going to change
my views, could you
stop doing this as i
have told you before
iam quite happy
without god in my
life !?
. .

On finding out the history to some notes, I can't help but thank God that I have flatmates who are very straightforward. When I received this one, the story that went with it made you thank anyone but God.

When this man (we shall call him 'Mr X') moved in, he seemed polite and posh, stating he was only going to be there for a year; the reason being he was engaged and did not want to live with his fiancée before they were married. An unusual decision perhaps, in this day and age, but the flatmates were fine with this arrangement. All seemed to be going OK, though Mr X did seem to talk about the importance of not living in sin a great deal and showed disdain when the other flatmates had their partners over to stay the night. The first photocopy of an excerpt from the Bible was treated by the flatmates as an oversight by Mr X – that he had simply left out something he was reading or studying. It wasn't until further photocopies started to appear and were finally pinned to the fridge that the flatmates realised that Mr X was on a mission of conversion. Things started to get nasty and apparently came to a head when a discussion about sex before marriage culminated with one of the exasperated flatmates asking, 'Well, how do you know you're compatible? She might have a weird rubber fetish.' Mr X was apparently very upset at this challenge, let alone the idea of his fiancée being into rubber and, soon after, he moved out. None of the flatmates were invited to the wedding.

Frank   Oh and another thing you have painted all the
        window shut and you will have to use a knife ▲

When I said could you clean the kitchen? I didn't
mean for you to Paint it!!

. You have just painted over everything including all the
dirt in white emulsion! It looks like a blizzard!
Do you not know how to clean cos this isn't the normal
way. The paint is already coming off the tiles and
the oven hood. I am going home for the weekend so
could you try and sort it out. You've been watching too much
                changing rooms! Stephanie

I was told in the letter accompanying this note that the issue of
cleaning was an argument waiting to happen. After a lot of hints
and attempts to cajole Frank into doing some housework he
eventually did it on quite a large scale. Frank described himself
as an 'all or nothing' character and this was the reason he gave
for the literal whitewashing of the cleaning. Using some old touch-
up paints that had been kicking around their flat for donkeys, he
covered every surface with paint. I am told the kitchen never
really got back to normal and every time a cloth was wiped over
a surface, white would come off. Stephanie eventually moved out.

Don't throw away. Ideal for 'beefing up' a risotto !!!

Contrary to what you might think, this note did not come out of wartime Britain. It was not from a decade hounded by rationing. It was left wrapped up in a small sandwich bag with two small ends of Parmesan in the fridge. Thoughtful, yet funny.

It can be very difficult to throw anything away. Due to an upbringing in which I was constantly being reminded to think of the starving in Africa, I could have lifted the pattern off a plate with my vigorous licking. I don't really know if the starving in Africa benefited from me being a fat, greedy child.

There is a recipe which all students embark on at some stage: tuna bake. Essentially, it is tuna and pasta with a 'golden crunchy topping'. This topping is basically a handful of crushed-up cornflakes. Why shards of dry tasteless cornflakes turn tuna pasta into a 'bake', I do not know, but it goes in the 'not wasting anything' category that students especially are fond of. My last ever attempt at frugal cooking was when I made a quiche using cheese slices that came wrapped in cellophane. Once cooked, the cheese went through some astonishing chemical change and became so tough I thought I had created some sort of new plastic. In fact, maybe it was through experiments with cheese during wartime that they discovered Bakelite?

Telephone Message

TIME RECEIVED_____   DATE_____

FROM_____

Mark,

        It really irritates me that when I come home from work late and all I want is a nice glass of orange juice that lo and behold my orange juice has been finished. As I have been working 14-hour days for the best part of 2 weeks whilst you have been "on the beach" waiting to be allocated onto a project perhaps you could buy your own bloody groceries.

RECEIVED BY_____

Neil

I know Neil – he is a lovely fellow with very good organisational skills. He is the kind of guy who uses ring reinforcements and copious amounts of highlighter pens. A hard-working conscientious guy, who I am told won the handwriting prize at school, as evident from this note. My heart therefore goes out to him. I do not think Neil is an 'economy range' kind of guy. You just know that this will have been one of those juices that aren't made from concentrate and probably cost more than liquid gold per litre. He has worked out how much juice he can have each day to make a carton last until the next shop. Long hours, sleep deprivation and Mark have got the better of him. Neil is not prone to emotional outbursts so this really must have been a juice too far.

Why is my bed damp?

LOVE, SEX, PARTNERS AND OTHER NOTES FROM THE BEDROOM

Creativity and the production of new ideas regularly happen in bedrooms. Apart from the most obvious form of creativity that can be performed there (*eeaasssy* now), reading, writing and of course listening to music are mainly done in this room. It is when this creativity seeps out of this room and into the general flat that very creative notes start appearing. The regular thumping noise of what you can only hope is your flatmate putting up shelves, but which you fear is something a bit more, well, physical, can ruin a good night's sleep. Equally, being tortured by the thudding of hardhouse techno at 2am when you are more of a Bob Dylan person can leave you feeling irascible and sleep deprived. The bedroom is meant to be a private space, but is not so in shared accommodation.

You never know what goes on behind closed doors, unless of course the doors and walls are paper thin. Living together shatters the illusion of any kind of domestic bliss. You are living out your relationships like a soap opera. This was one of the driving factors behind this book. As a long-suffering flat-sharer, I am an experienced voyeur of people's lives. I've watched the ups and the downs, and seen the seemingly perfect often quickly unravel with slams, grunts and raised voices. To keep up any kind of pretence in the confinements of a flat is almost impossible, but that doesn't stop most people trying to crack smiles as though they never heard a thing as they pass each other in the hall. For these reasons flat-sharing can be a very good test of a relationship. It bodes well if you can cope with a judge and jury while you are being your most irrational and grumpy, and when your behaviour generally leaves a lot to be desired.

However it is also difficult if you are single. Try wooing a new beau when there are not two but three of you squeezed together on the sofa. Or maybe the new squeeze fancies your flatmate too and before you know it you are in a sordid three-way relationship, taking one from people you only live with because you need help paying the rent. Terrible.

The bedroom should be a sanctuary – a place to relax and escape your troubles. This is easier said than done, though, when you realise someone else has been relaxing on your bed and left their dirty kegs as a fragrant reminder.

Carla

You seem to be
very busy during
the night.

Unfortunately, I'm very
busy during the
day and use the
night to sleep.
So can you consider
keeping the noise
down — or getting
a day job ?

Thanks. Jo x

Some of the notes that have come to me with no explanation attached are the best. Carla's busy late-night schedule makes the mind boggle.

don't put too much on me.
I'm delicate

This is very clever. Effectively you are now rendered utterly mute. Discuss or complain about anything and this person may dissolve into an emotional mess. This note is a giant get-out clause that the sender can quote back to you. They might as well cover the floor with eggshells and be done with it. That said, it could be that I am reading far too much into this, for it could be about something much simpler, namely, a table. Though this is possible, it would be a bit fucking weird to start writing notes on behalf of inanimate objects.

Dear ███,

███ ██ tells me that you are angry at not being introduced to my boyfriend ███

I'm sorry if I have not done this but I thought I had already – as I made sure the ███ knew a long time ago (when ██ █ was being threatened by Jamaican Yardies. I didn't want him to worry about seeing my Jamaican boyfriend in the flat) and I must have missed you out.

You haven't been in the flat much over the past few months, but if you are around sometime when you think ███ might be here please feel free to knock on my door + I can put this right and introduce you.

I also gave my spare set of keys to ███ recently as he lives on the other side of London in ████████ + was arriving here at stupid times in the morning (2 or 3 am) and I didn't want him ringing the doorbell and waking everyone up. However if you feel at all uncomfortable about this just say the word and I'll take them back. I'm sorry he has startled you.

TAKE CARE ███

Oh, for the love of God, this is complex. So there is a stranger walking around the flat that you have never met – potentially disconcerting – but this writer seems to have a guilty conscience and has jumped a few steps ahead. They seem to be stating their boyfriend is *not* in a gang – did anyone think he was? I am sure they do now after this note. I don't know if this guy should go out with this girl any more because:

a)   She seems to presume everyone will think he is a gangster because he is Jamaican.

b)   If he is a gangster, she is making everyone very suspicious and doing a good job of blowing his cover.

i'm not good at saying this so I wont, I'll write it. Sorry!

This is one of my favourite notes. The main reason is that it is actually written on the back of a prescription. Not a good sign. This could be the start of a lot of sorry notes. Pass the Valium.

I am sure this is meant to be a lovely note but I can feel bile gathering in my throat. Not so much because of the saccharine-sweet sentiment but for anyone else who has to live with this warring and 'making up' pair. I bet they have nicknames for each other. Alternatively, these are two men who have found they can express their inner self by putting on make-up. This is in fact a bloody good idea – a make-up school specifically for blokes who have got into wearing frilly pants and mascara. I'm off to write the course now.

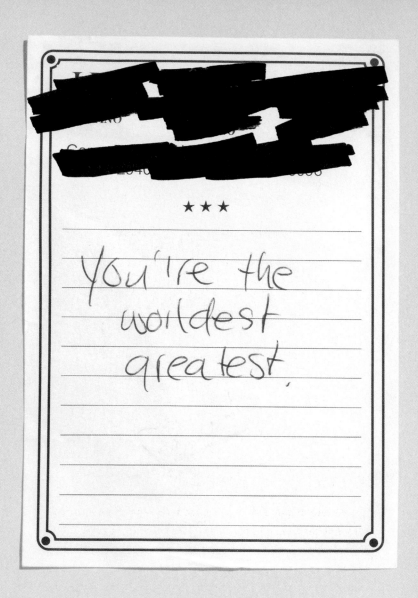

★ ★ ★

You're the
worldest
greatest.

To get a note like this is the bestest everest!

Hi there cute buns!
Do you come here often?
.... oh you live here

— lucky old me
Kx

Inter-flatmate flirting can be very good fun, as this note demonstrates, but can also be horrific if you're the gooseberry in the middle not receiving any of the notes. You can be left feeling awkward in your own living space, or convinced that as soon as you leave a room there is something going on. There is also the terrible threat of 'lucky old them' suddenly thinking 'cute buns' is crap – then you feel even more awkward because the only thing happening when you leave the room is a huge argument.

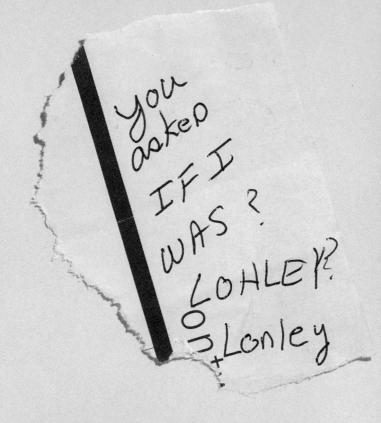

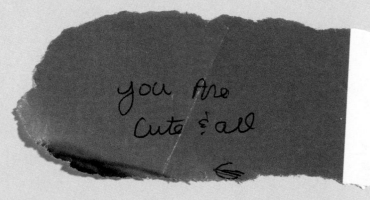

In US
There ARe
LoTS Like
Me

This seems to be a series of love notes in very broken English answering some rather creepy questions. Where are there 'lots like me'? Why are they asking if they are lonely? Who is asking these questions? It sounds like a rather strange stalker, sorry, flatmate.

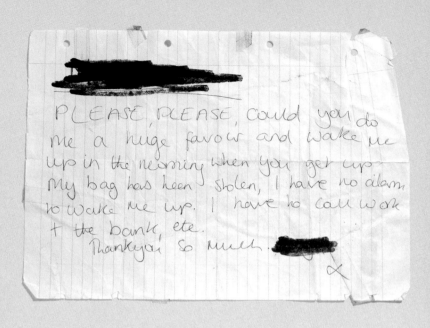

PLEASE, PLEASE, could you do me a huge favour and wake me up in the morning when you get up. My bag has been stolen, I have no alarm to wake me up. I have to call work + the bank, etc.
Thankyou so much ■■■■
x

The recipient of this note has been turned into the role of parent and counsellor, having to look after and clear up after the shambolic flatmate. Problem is, when you are in this situation you have no choice, as you know the one time you do not wake them up, they will sleep in, be late for work, lose their job, and end up drunk and penniless on the street.

I have put your copy of
'My Wammys are bigger than
                                    Pammy's
in your bedroom.

Yes, it's one thing for young men to watch porn videos, it is another to leave them in the video recorder for their female flatmates to find. The lady who wrote this note said she made sure that she left the note out for all to see.

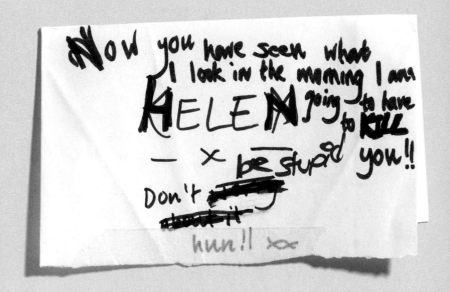

A very funny note. It could simply be that Helen was a little dishevelled, panda-eyed and bedraggled, but I think it is much more entertaining that maybe, just maybe, she was not only bedraggled but starkers! Being caught in the buff by a flatmate, or anyone else for that matter who you are not romantically linked to, is very embarrassing. It is often made worse by the element of surprise. With no warning, you do not have time to tense muscles and strike a flattering pose. Instead, you are generally hopping around putting one leg into underwear, rear aloft, drying toes, or in some other unglamorous position. As you hear the rather shocked viewer scuttling off giggling embarrassedly, you can only wish that you could kill them, wipe their memory or at the very least pray they believe beauty is not skin deep.

So so sorry!!

thought you were away
for the w/end.... so wouldn't
mind my sister staying in
you bed. She said you looked
a mixture of frightened &
pleased to find a strange
woman in your bed when you
came in! <u>really</u> sorry, & it
was very kind of you to
offer to sleep on the sofa

The young gentleman in this note didn't know if his Christmases had all come at once, or if he should call the police. He arrived home very late to find a young lady safely tucked up in his bed in her underwear. Both were equally shocked to see each other and there then followed some very awkward, quick explanations and apologies. It did not help that it was late, dark and both were sleepy. The young lady exited the bed to sleep in the living room. She was not the result of our gentleman rubbing a lamp, but the visiting sister of his flatmate. Now nicknamed 'Goldilocks', she has opted not to stay again but to get the night bus home before she gets a reputation.

Hi   , I feel I should explain my
odd behaviour last night When I came
in I wasn't sure if THAT was the bloke
you had talked about — so didn't know
the 'situation'. Because I thought I had
just walked in on something, I was
embarrassed and in trying to act
calm cool and really normal I
think I just came across as really
wierd X

not for sale

Living with others can mean you become embroiled in each other's problems and relationships. A night in front of the television can quickly become a counselling session. Whether you like it or not you tend to know more than you would like to about people that you live with. This is especially odd as they might not necessarily be people you would have chosen to be friends with. This poor soul has come home from a day at work and suddenly had to work out all sorts of unspoken dynamics. It can be very difficult to pick up on subtle emotional nuances and, in your desperation not to put the proverbial foot in it, you can come across as cold, enigmatic, or worse, just plain stupid. Suddenly when asked simple questions, you have no idea how to answer. 'Do you live here?' 'I don't know, do I?'

I pray that this is simply something like a window has been left open, or a helpful flatmate has washed the bedding and it is still slightly moist. Yet I can't help thinking there is something much much darker behind this note.

DATE.
TODAY

SIGNED.
A FRIEND

Hi ~~████~~ was out @ the union last
night and saw Pete with some blond —
Seemed to leave with her !! He was
pretty pissed. Hope it is all innocent;
(possibly his sister?) Sorry to be the
bringer of bad news if it wasn't.
Call if you need to chat

There are some people who you can't help suspecting enjoy
being the bringer of bad tidings. They always seem to know
everyone's business and are in the centre of every drama. Their
sentences often start with 'I don't want to be a gossip' or 'I'm
not being a bitch', before swiftly turning to something bitchy or
scandalous. A faux confidant is a dangerous person. When they
ask you how you are or how you feel, with a helpful arm around
you, they are working out the quickest way to report your demise
to every corner of the world. Poor Millie, the last person she
would have wanted to witness this possible philandering is the
local gossip Jane.

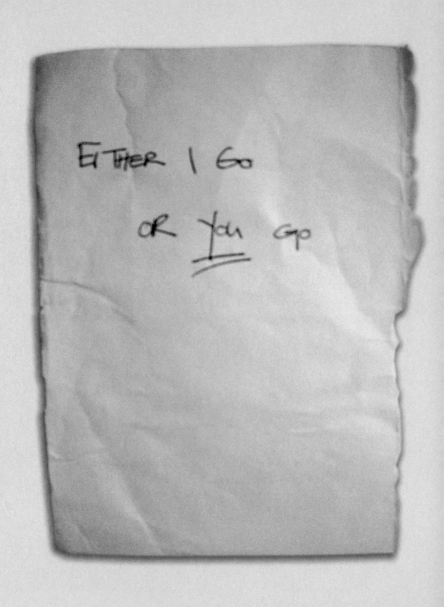

I am guessing that this note is not quite as it seems. I am basing this presumption on a flat story I was told involving a cute cat. My friend said that he moved in with a group of friends and their very lovely kitten. Things were good at first but very quickly the sneezing and itching started. Yes, my friend was allergic to the cat. My friend said that it got to the point where, like in this note, it became obvious that they could not live together and one of them had to go. Somewhat inevitably, it was my friend who became the stray and had to find allergy-free accommodation. He also pointed out that if I did not believe the severity of his problems, he would show me his prescriptions for an array of antihistamines. Thus, I hope this note is about someone who is allergic to dumb dogs. I know I find it hard to stay in the same room as a stupid bitch.

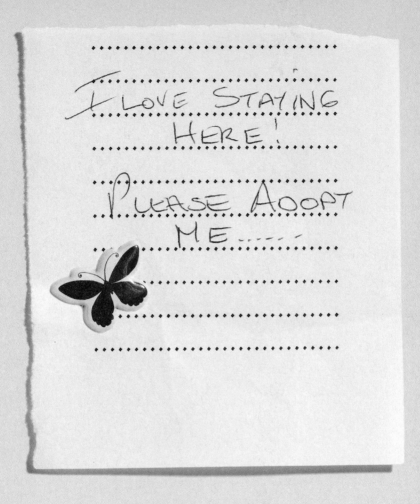

Though this is an endearing note, feeling like you're the parent of a flatmate is not a good situation to find yourself in. It is one thing doing the dishes or putting the rubbish out, but where does it stop? Making their tea? Blowing their nose? Adopting a child is a very difficult decision to make, though many of us end up adopting adults not really having made a choice at all. Grow up!

Have you moved your boyfriend in? We have been discussing that he is here most nights. Should we have a flat meeting?

Hugs, Gatsby xx

This is that transition point in a relationship. You like each other enough to want to see each other most nights but are not ready to live together. It comes after about a year and can be a make-or-break moment. If you love each other so much, why the reluctance to share the same space? Eventually, there has to be a discussion about the issues. In this case, the discussion has been hurried along by the other flatmates. The horror of a flat meeting is enough to make you run to the hills. The use of the word 'we' also sows the seeds of paranoia in your head. Have they all been discussing you and your boyfriend? Why? Don't they like him? It might be better to face living with the boyfriend than face the flat meeting.

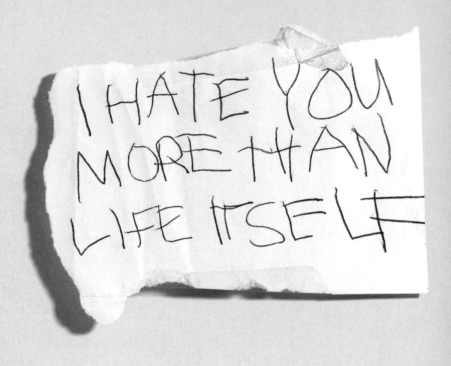

What the hell did the recipient of this note do to deserve it? Or rather, what didn't they do? Or were they completely innocent? Well, when I study this note closely it looks as though it has been stuck to a wall or door. Hmm, determined. In these kinds of scenarios, it is better just to have a large supply of 'sorry' notelets to hand as trying to work out what on earth the problem is could in itself push this note writer over the edge.

We seem to be physically . together but mentally apart! We are living this together. I am here for you man feel free to share. Peace D!

Amazingly this note was written in the twenty-first century and not on the back of an acid tab in 1973. Peace.

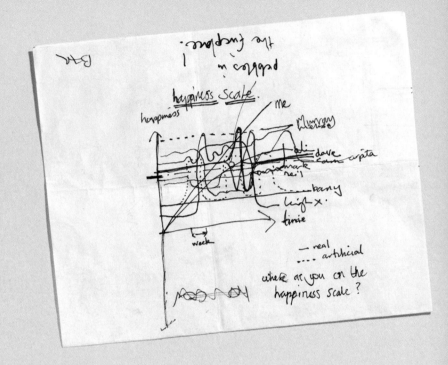

Sitting down and actually working out your levels of happiness can be very therapeutic and revealing. Are you happier, happiest or hoping to be happy. On this graph, some are off the scale while others are still in the negative numbers. This is one of the most creative submissions and one I look forward to seeing in psychiatric textbooks in years to come.

HOSTILE COMUNICATION

SUN 26 —— MARCH

TAT ~~■■■~~ ARNE

|| /||| ~~HH|~~

SUN 2/4/06

|| (| | | |

HOUSE MEETING ~~Postponed~~
8 -15 .   DONT BE LATE.
ON LOVE ISLAND (ie RED)

I have met these two and they are a lovely couple who live together. They have devised a system that I think all couples should use: a 'nice scale'. It is a visual tool to show when either of them have been, well, a tool. Every harsh word or unreasonable action is represented by a black mark against the inflictor's name. Looking closely at this picture, I think Arne is due to buy Tat some flowers very soon. I am not quite sure if there were any actual penalties incurred if you got a certain amount of 'not nice' points, but I would have thought the fact you could see it on a board would be enough to make you change your ways. There is also the question of what amounts to 'not nice' and this again depends on people's standards. I was once questioned by one of my prolific note-writing flatmates as to what it would take before I wrote a note to her. I thought about it for some time before saying if she peed on the floor that might upset me. Unfortunately, this concept and my rather crass turn of phrase made her write a long note about the conversation. It was a real no-win situation. She was sensitive, I was not. I'm sure my 'not nice' column would have been maxed out.

Thank
you for
everything
you did
for me
& for
being
you ♡

Have you ever thought that if you dropped down dead not only would nobody notice but also they would probably step over you? They don't care so you won't care. This can lead to a grim outlook on mankind. This is when you get your elbows out when shopping, don't give change to buskers (and sometimes even kick their dog) and positively hate anyone who cracks a smile. There are times when you just want to curl up under a duvet with a Valium, or sit on the sofa scoffing at losers on reality TV. It is just at these points in your life when you hate yourself and everyone around you that a note like this can mean the world. The cynic in me wants to make all sorts of retching noises and talk about the nauseating sweetness of this note, but it is too easy to mock. Fact is, I'd like to think it wasn't easy to write it. In any event, as a recipient it's good to think that not only have you done something kind and not had it gobbed back in your face, but you have done something kind that didn't put you through hell and back – you just had to be yourself. A 'thank you' or a 'love you', or a note like this is enough to make you emerge blinking like Gollum from out of the bedclothes, put down the barbiturates, turn off Simon Cowell, shave and start viewing life a bit more positively. We all have duvet days and the fact that you managed to help someone out of their depression should help you out of yours. I think if someone gave me this note I would keep it in my pocket, so when a shopper had just elbowed me and all felt hopeless, I would remember that it was OK just being me.

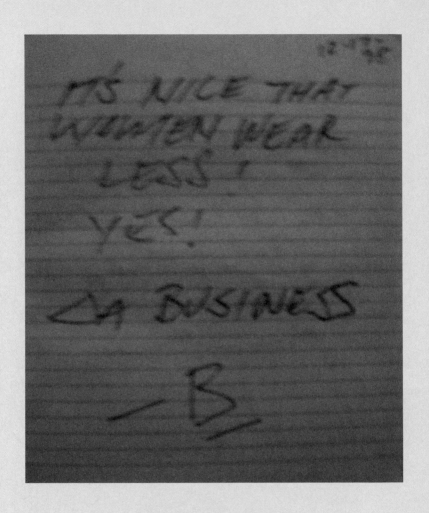

That someone was compelled to write this note is almost touching. What vision, what demi-goddess did they see that meant that by the time they arrived in their home they needed to make a public announcement? And wear less – less than what? Before? Themselves? 'Da business' doesn't sound like it comes from someone who has just arrived from a land where women are covered head to toe. Or maybe this person has gone through a late puberty – the scales have just dropped from their eyes and they're suddenly acutely aware of every curve on every female. I happen to know this was written by a male (before anyone writes in saying this could have been a lesbian). I don't know him, but I feel I have seen him – he is one of those young dudes who even if you were wearing four layers of thermals and a balaclava would still be able to 'undress you with his eyes'. So maybe this is his point. He has realised that women are wearing less and less clothing, which means he has to do less undressing with his eyes. This adds a lazy lustre. I should maybe give him a tip: nobody likes a lazy lover, no matter how little clothing they have on.

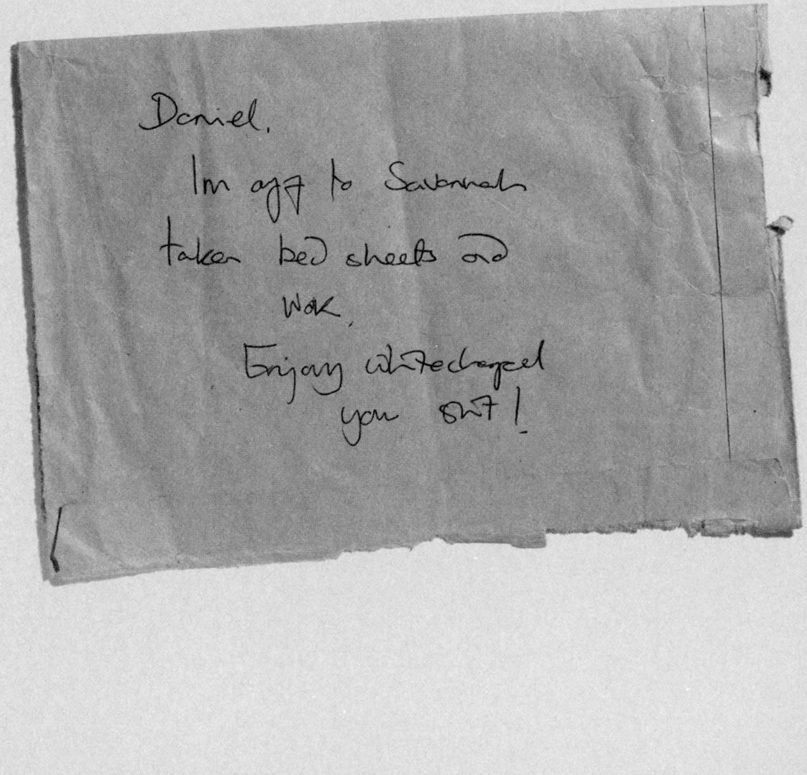
Daniel,
taken bed sheets and
wok.
Enjoy whitechapel

This cohabiting pair are actually very loving and the tension of the situation, I suspect, got the better of them. Living with a couple can cause lots of conflicts, especially if you find yourself taking sides, not taking sides or having to do whatever is appropriate/inappropriate. It is particularly difficult when opportunities turn up such as jobs which could involve a move abroad. This gives rise to tricky conversations, and a shift from a casual relationship and just seeing what will happen to being forced into putting your cards on the table. How do you see this panning out? Are you coming with me or am I going to go without you? I hear this couple went to Savannah together in the end, where I am happy to say they are still sharing their wok.

Hi Beck, It was a complete DISASTER. I'm sure Neil is a really nice bloke but he spent the whole time talking about his CRUCIAL LIGAMENT OPERATION that GAZZA had?? In really graphic detail. He then told me about all the exercises he had to do (with a demonstration in the pub!) and explained that he could have been in the Premier League. Told him I preferred RUGBY! Oh well, it was nice to get a few free DRINKS!!

Hold on, hold on, let me get this right. This bloke is trying to win the affection of this young filly by telling her about an operation he had had? Even more astounding – is he comparing himself to Gazza? Is this the same Gazza otherwise known as Paul Gascoigne, who allegedly beat up his wife, sang 'Fog on the Tyne is all mine, all mine' in a shell suit and dyed his hair blue? Good grief, how can she not be tempted? Surely she must be a big old lezza to turn down this cad.

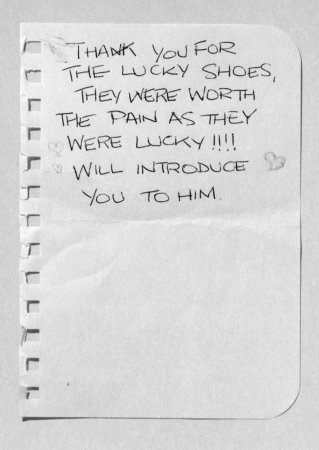

THANK YOU FOR THE LUCKY SHOES, THEY WERE WORTH THE PAIN AS THEY WERE LUCKY !!!! WILL INTRODUCE YOU TO HIM.

Doesn't David Beckham have, like, loads of lucky shit that he wears? I don't mean literally, though I think if I had a Beckham poo I would be lucky, as I could probably flog it on eBay for some insane price. Lots of people flog their pants I have heard. In Japan, you can buy young girls' used pants from vending machines. I prefer Mars Bars.

HI PETE

HAVE HAD TO GO OUT, BUT I HAVE GOT YOUR PHONE
CHARGER IN MY ROOM MY ONE DOESN'T SEEM TO
BE WORKING. PHONE PACKED UP IN THE MIDDLE
OF A MASSIVE FIGHT WITH HALEY AND SHE
THOUGHT I PUT THE PHONE DOWN ON HER, SO
OFF TO USE THE PHONE BOX AND TRY TO EXPLAIN
EXPLAIN WHAT HAPPENED. FOR THE FIRST TIME IT
ISN'T A LAME EXCUSE...

Oh deary me! 'Massive fight', 'put the phone down', 'lame excuse'
– these are not phrases I would expect to see in a message
about a happy relationship. I think this young man might have
given his last 'lame excuse' to Hayley. Unless the grovelling in
the phone box melts Hayley's cold and now suspicious heart,
then the note writer need not bother charging his phone. All that
will happen is that when he switches on the phone he will have
several missed calls and a voicemail saying he is a wanker.

Dear ▓▓▓▓▓

Our phone bill has been very large since you moved in. I don't think we should split it as I have noticed in the itemising a lot of 0898 numbers being called at night and I don't think we should pay for your expensive "hobbie"!!

▓▓▓▓

It's a bit weird when you find out someone you know is a bit of a perv. It goes into the same category as finding out that someone you think is really cool and interesting likes wine bars and Kenny G.

Being a perv is OK if you make it apparent from the start – you know, gimp-masked up, rubber pants and asking to be whipped – but being caught off guard can be really confusing. When a friend of mine went to get her nose pierced, a guy in a very sensible suit came in, ripped open his shirt and tie and got his nipples pierced. Again, that's just confusing. If I go to the post office I don't want to start wondering if the old lady behind the desk is actually wearing anything below that desk. Ah, but I suppose it is that element of surprise that is half the perversion. Obvious perversions (ie trying to shock) become a bit dull – a case in point being teenagers dressed as goths. (Honestly get over it, no one cares about your adolescent angst and your craply-made goth gear.) Essentially, this 0898 caller doesn't sound like a perv but just bored. I think he actually gets turned on by these notes. He probably doesn't even listen to the dirty dialogue because he's too busy getting off on the notes from this angry lady.

James —

Just gone round
to Safeways to
pick up some
shopping.

Lots of love
Tifs

Who on earth is called Tits? And more to the point, who refers to *themselves* as Tits? Is this one of those weird girls you can hire to do the housework? I didn't know they would go to the shops naked. Surely that's just dangerous. Never mind the swerving oncoming traffic, think of the chafing from the seatbelt on poor Tits. Hold on, have I misread this? Are they going shopping for 'love tits'? What are love tits? Where can you buy these love tits? Maybe they are simply those sidesplitting breast-shaped chocolates you can buy at the back of card shops in empty shopping malls. Unfortunately, I know the background to these two. No, they are not buying any special chocolates or sex toys. Anita, whose nickname is 'Tita', wrote the note. Amusingly, when this is written in a rush on the way to going to the shops the 'a' looks distinctly like an 's', and suddenly Tita is Tits. Before you ask, yes, Tita has got a big chest.

Hi Alan, Arsehole in the room next door said he went into my room to get some of my magazines to put under his door to stop the draught?! He looked well embarrassed when he was telling me. He is obviously talking bull I know he's been laying on my bed again.. He's well strange

28

This note is awful on so many levels. It starts with a truly baffling excuse which must have taken some time to digest and understand as it is obviously a lie. The fact that 'arsehole' is lying on the bed *again* is the terrifying bit and that elaborate explanations are being constructed to cover it up. This makes you think he is not innocently reading on the bed. The next worry is does he secretly want you to know that he lies on your bed? Strange is the biggest understatement about this individual.

Yesterday when I found you going through my drawers and you said that you were looking for your paint... I think I was in shock just to see you in my room. Now when I think about it why were you in my room? And why if I did have your paint would I keep it in my underwear drawer? KEEP OUT OF MY ROOM you creep, I'm putting a lock on my door and anything like this is harrasment and I will call the police.

Another moment of clarity. Sometimes, when someone tells you a brazen lie you are in such shock you just take it on board. As this note points out, it is only later that the pieces of the jigsaw come together. The warning bells must have started going off when she realised that out of every area of the room it was the underwear drawer that was his first port of call.

This is a NON smoking flat
& that includes in the bedrooms
even if you do smoke out the window!

I think it is only a matter of time before I write a book about
flat deaths. We have had eggs exploding, plastic melting and
potentially people falling out of windows having a sly fag. It is
true that smoking may kill you, but just quicker than you think
if you keep hanging out of windows.

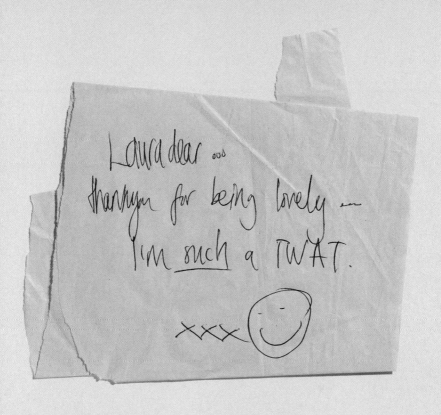

No explanation needed.

Afterword

This book may be coming to a conclusion, but the trials and tribulations of living with others are neverending while you're renting. We are the little people: the people who don't buy *Homes and Gardens* magazine because we don't have either; the people who have been saved from the hell of Ikea as the place we live in is not ours to decorate. We are the Renters – the ones stuck in limbo with no property ladder to hang on to. That said, the security of your own place often takes away the chance of sharing with a bunch of randoms. Whichever way you look at it, sharing your space with others makes you stronger and more interesting whether you like it or not.

We humans seem to be unsure whether we are better off as individual creatures who are meant to have their own little cave to shuffle around in, or as pack animals wanting to groom, eat and generally hang out together. The Internet reflects this ambiguity. You can guarantee those who are keenest on making virtual friends have distinctly fewer friends in the real world. Yes, the *real* world.

The best bit about compiling this book has been the people I have met or talked about. You can't help feeling you know or have met someone similar when you read the notes. Sometimes, just sometimes, you cringe as you recognise yourself. C'mon, admit it. The book has forced me to look at my own weird habits, and though I don't have Obsessive-Compulsive Disorder, I do have 'a friend' who can't go to bed if they think the ornaments in the living room are not lined up straight. OK, that's right, the straight ornaments will make everything better.

If you have taken to eating your dinner in the locked bathroom to avoid social interaction in your flat, then this may be the perfect tactful gift for the nemesis you have ended up living with. Just leave the book on their bed, open at the relevant page. Unlike most communication today, the notes are mainly written by hand (as opposed to typed). The choice of paper and the writing provide ample material for analysis, and for that reason the book has become almost like a counselling session. It can be cathartic to find out there are people in more fucked-up situations than you. Take solace from the book. Sit back and ponder why some of these people live together or how some of them manage to live at all.

On the other hand, if you have got to the end of this book and felt that you have notes that make these pale into insignificance, you still have an opportunity to let the world know by adding your notes to the website (www.flatmatesanonymous.com). Surely that would be the sweetest revenge of all. Not only that, but if you visit the website you might meet people that you actually like! Along with adding or viewing notes, you could also get some advice on your own flat-share situation. And if all else fails, you could try advertising for a new flatmate on the site. You might find the perfect match. For example: Wanted, a flatmate who doesn't leave crusty pants in the bathroom, but just cleans it. Yes, find a new flatmate from the website – at least you know you like reading the same books!

To conclude, during my research I came across several university sites offering help and guidance on living together. My favourite was run by the Swinburne College Australia (www.swinburne.edu.au).

To quote the site:

How to share successfully

In order to make sharing a success, you need to establish your house rules with those with whom you will be sharing. Some important considerations when seeking shared accommodation are:

- *cost*
- *number of people in the household and their ages*
- *male/female ratio*
- *proximity to campus and public transport*
- *special dietary requirements such as vegetarianism*
- *smokers-Non-smokers in the household*
- *cultural differences*
- *common interests of those in the household*

Great advice, except not all of us are sensible, mature, rational and selfless individuals. With the best will in the world, living with others will always have its ups and downs, but it is preferable to living as a hermit, growing long fingernails and weeing in bottles. How boring life would be if you did follow these rules, and how little you would appreciate your own space if you always had it.

Acknowledgements

Just before I sign off to set up my own virtual flat, eat virtual pies and watch virtual porn with virtually no mates, there are a few people I would like to thank.

Thank you to family and friends, but more so to foes! The foes gave me the impetus to get this book underway and exorcise their demons from my memory. Thank you to many of my students for their input. Thank you, Alan D, who I would always be happy to live with again. Big, big thank you to Adelaide for generally lots of things and helping with the book – I miss finding you milling around the living room. Extremely large and neverending thank you to Mr M Young – my favourite 'flatmate' in the world. Thank you to Gordon Wise and to everyone at Little Brown, especially Antonia Hodgson.